A Book of
Blessings

Publications International, Ltd.

Contents

Enriching Our Lives

Prayer is just talking to God——sharing our hopes, our dreams, our fears, and our heartaches with the only one who understands us completely. God yearns to be close to us, to be a part of our lives. God wants us to turn to him whenever we feel weak, scared, or alone, and need someone who can help us.

There is no right way to pray. Some of the most beautiful prayers are the most simple in language. Prayers can be whispered, put into song, shouted out to the heavens, or simply said in one's heart. It is always an appropriate time to pray.

We pray whenever we create space in our day to share with God. We pray with our words, but we can also pray without words. For God not only knows our minds, but he sees the depths of our hearts. He sees us as we truly are, so he always knows what we need.

You may wish to spend a few relaxing moments with this book on a hectic day, reading through a prayer or two alone, during a time of quiet. At other times you might need several soothing prayers to ease your weary, troubled mind. In either case, remember that prayer is both an action and an attitude.

Let this book remind you to pause for a moment and know that God is near. In moments of praise and thanksgiving or in moments of hardship and despair, God's Word holds true: "I am with you always." The blessings we receive every day serve as a reminder of this divine promise.

Chapter 1

Love

And now abideth faith, hope, charity, these three; but the greatest of these is charity.

1 Corinthians 13:13

Love 7

Charity suffereth long, and is kind; charity envieth not; charity vaunteth not itself, is not puffed up,

Doth not behave itself unseemly, seeketh not her own, is not easily provoked, thinketh no evil;

Rejoiceth not in iniquity, but rejoiceth in the truth;

Beareth all things, believeth all things, hopeth all things, endureth all things.

1 Corinthians 13:4–7

God, it's a quiet day. Help me pause to listen to you, to talk to you, to enjoy your company. Chase away my guilt and shame and fear, and draw me close to your heart. Remind me that no matter what my earthly roles may be, in your presence I am your child, and you care for me more than I could ever imagine. Let me lean against your heart now, Father, and hear it beating with love for me. Amen.

*L*ord, grant me a simple, kind, open, believing, loving and generous heart, worthy of being your dwelling place.

~~~~~~~~~~~~~~~~

*G*od in heaven above,
 Bless me with your love.
Send your angel choir to guide me.
Safe within your arms, please hide me.
High in heaven's dome,
I'll make your heart my home.

*Open wide the window of our spirits, O Lord,
and fill us full of light;
Open wide the door of our hearts, that we may
receive and entertain thee with all our powers of
adoration and love.*

–Christina Rossetti

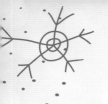

But I have trusted in thy mercy;
my heart shall rejoice in thy salvation.

Psalm 13:5

*L*ord above, you look down upon us, and still you
love us. When we look down on others, it is because we
are angered and cannot see their points of view. We also
still love them, but sometimes our anger clouds our love.
Please help us stay grounded and find understanding.
Amen.

*D*ear Father, help me to see that I sometimes
amplify the bad times because I push others away and
become selfish. Please teach me to love. Amen.

*W*hen I am having a bad day, and the last thing I want to do is love, I love anyway. This is when God calls upon me the most to get out of my bubble and give comfort to someone else who might need it. In turn, I begin to feel more loving, towards myself, towards others, and towards humanity. God knows that the best way to find the love we seek is to give it.

*G*od comforts me with his love when I am feeling cold and alone. God warms me with his loving care when I am feeling neglected. God sees me when I am feeling unseen, and reminds me of my worth when I am feeling inadequate. God's love is my comfort in all things, and it makes me whole again.

You love us Lord, not because we are particularly lovable. And it's certainly not the case that you need to receive our love. I am so heartened by this: You offer your love simply because you delight to do it.

Behold, what manner of love the Father hath bestowed upon us, that we should be called the sons of God: therefore the world knoweth us not, because it knew him not.

1 John 3:1

How often do we let time drift by without telling those we hold dear to us how much we love them? How often do we fear speaking words of love because we might be rejected? If only we could possibly know just how much we are loved, by each other, and by God. We would then know that miracles truly exist and all things are possible. Love gives us wings. Tell someone you love them today.

I love the Lord, because he hath
heard my voice and my supplications.
Because he hath inclined his ear unto me,
therefore will I call upon him as long as I live.

Psalm 116:1–2

To think
You think
Of me!
How great!
How great
You are,
I think!
I ask;
You give
What
You think
Best.
How great
You are,
I think!

Lord, dismiss us with thy blessing,
Hope, and comfort from above;
Let us each, thy peace possessing,
Triumph in redeeming love.

– Robert Hawker

God, make me an open vessel through which the waters of your Spirit flow freely. Let your love move through me and out into my world, touching everyone I come in contact with. Express your joy through the special talents you have given me, that others may come to know your presence in their own lives by witnessing your presence in mine. Amen.

Lord, I'm glad you are merciful and gracious. Today I'm resting in your steadfast love, and in your hugs. Amen.

*And above all things have fervent charity
among yourselves: for charity shall cover
the multitude of sins.*

1 Peter 4:8

*God! Thou art love! I build my faith on that...
I know thee, who hast kept my path, and made
Light for me in darkness, tempering sorrow
So that it reached me like a solemn joy;
It were too strange that I should doubt thy love.*

–Robert Browning, "Paracelsus"

*I believe, God, that you give us faith as a means
of getting in touch with your love.
For once we have that love, we can pass it
on to others.*

–Henry Drummond

*C*ount neither the hours nor the seconds
That filled your mind with doubts and fears.
Do not add up unhappy moments,
When pain and hardships brought you to tears.
Regard not days on faded calendars
That marked the passage of your years.
Instead, count heaven's blessings...
Grandchildren playing on the floor,
Old friends walking through the door,
White clouds drifting up above,
And, like a faithful timepiece, God's love.

I will sing unto the Lord, because he hath dealt bountifully with me.

Psalm 13:6

⌇⌇⌇⌇⌇⌇⌇⌇⌇⌇⌇⌇⌇

If I count the things I've asked for that you have not given me, I begin to believe you do not love me, God. But if, instead, I bring to mind all of the goodness you have shown me, I come to trust that you have never given me less than what I need and often have blessed me with far more from a depth of love I cannot comprehend.

Let thy mercy, O Lord, be upon us,
according as we hope in thee.

Psalm 33:22

*L*ord, we want to live life to its fullest. And although we know we shouldn't place our own wants before others' wants, it is so easy to think our dreams for the future matter most. Remind us to make compromises. Our love can get us further in this life than selfishness. Amen.

*G*od Almighty, thank you for the people that inspire me to accept others. Let me learn to love everyone—including myself. Amen.

The first time I saw you, I loved you more than I could say.
Little did I realize then, I would love you more each day.

When joy and laughter vanish
Into illness and despair,
I remind myself that with God's help
You can get there from here.
So let not doubt and fear take seed
And grow into a tree,
But let God's healing make me whole
And love take root in me.

As the Father hath loved me,
so have I loved you: continue ye in my love.

If ye keep my commandments,
ye shall abide in my love; even as I have
kept my Father's commandments, and
abide in his love.

John 15:9–10

*L*ove. It seems so simple. Love is a gift given. Yet, if we don't overlook it, Lord, we treat it like a gift certificate saved so long it expires. We are down-on-our-knees grateful your gifts of love and grace never expire. Nudge us to use them, for we lose their value each day they go unclaimed. We stay disconnected from you, the source of creation and re-creation. To connect only requires a "Yes!" from us. Hear us shout!

A new commandment I give unto you,
That ye love one another; as I have loved
you, that ye also love one another.

By this shall all men know that ye are my
disciples, if ye have love one to another.

John 13:34–35

Father, unity among your people is precious to you—and precious to us as well. We cannot achieve it without your assistance, though. Help us to keep petty disagreements from dividing us. Give us the grace to work through any disagreement with love and understanding.

*With all lowliness and meekness,
with longsuffering, forbearing one another in love;
Endeavouring to keep the unity of the Spirit
in the bond of peace.*

Ephesians 4:2–3

*F*ather, help us to touch and influence others. We want them to recognize and celebrate even the small blessings. We want to surprise them with gestures of love. Amen.

*L*ord, thank you for bringing others into our lives to help us heal. We appreciate how much they aid us. Please remind us to thank them for reaching out to us. Thank you for extending your love to us through them. Amen.

$\mathcal{A}$s we learn to trust you, God, we discover your strengthening presence in various places and people. Wherever we encounter shelter, comfort, rest, and peace, we are bound to hear your voice, welcoming us. And in whomever we find truth, love, gentleness, and humility, we are sure to hear your heartbeat, assuring us that you will always be near. Thank you, God. Amen.

$\mathcal{H}$eavenly Father, you are the author of love. We are able to love only because you first loved us. You taught us how to love you and each other—our family and our neighbors. We want everyone to know your perfect love, and we invite the fragrance of your love to permeate our home.

So let all thine enemies perish, O
Lord: but let them that love him be
as the sun when he goeth forth in
his might. And the land had rest
forty years.

Judges 5:31

Oh, the deep, deep love of Jesus,
Vast unmeasured, boundless free;
Rolling as a mighty ocean
In its fullness over me.
Underneath me, all around me,
Is the current of Thy love;
Leading onward, leading homeward,
To my glorious rest above.

—Samuel T. Francis

But as it is written, Eye hath not seen, nor ear heard, neither have entered into the heart of man, the things which God hath prepared for them that love him.

1 Corinthians 2:9

*F*ather, nothing moves me more to love others than reflecting on how you love me. I think of all the things you could have held against me and used as reasons to not love me. And yet you always look for ways to forgive, restore our relationship, and move forward. I want to love like that!

Thy mercy, O Lord, is in the heavens;
and thy faithfulness reacheth unto the clouds.

Thy righteousness is like the great mountains;
thy judgments are a great deep: O Lord, thou
preservest man and beast.

How excellent is thy lovingkindness, O God!
therefore the children of men put their trust
under the shadow of thy wings.

Psalm 36:5–7

I know yours is a persistent devotion, Lord. Your devoted love for me is the example that helps me to love others as well. What would I prefer to your love? What could I love more than those I hold dear? Nothing in the universe! Who are the loves of my life? Let me count them all and delight in them today.

Father, when I don't have another ounce of strength to give, you give me gallons of love to fuel my spirit. When I think I can't continue, you push me further and steady my steps. Thank you, God.

Beloved, let us love one another:
for love is of God; and every one that loveth
is born of God, and knoweth God.

He that loveth not knoweth not
God; for God is love.

In this was manifested the love of
God toward us, because that God sent his only
begotten Son into the world, that we might
live through him.

Herein is love, not that we loved God,
but that he loved us, and sent his Son to be the
propitiation for our sins.

1 John 4:7–10

*F*ather, it's to you we come,
To pray for loved ones and for friends;
You offer mercy, grace, and peace,
And healing love that never ends.

*L*ift up thine eyes to see the light
that heals the sick and makes wrongs right.
Lift up thine heart to feel the love
that emanates from God above.

*W*here God is, our comfort and hope is. The divine
presence blesses us when we walk in his light and do his
will. We are bearers of light and love to all those we meet.
We are his divinely inspired earthbound angels.

*Many waters cannot quench love, neither
can the floods drown it: if a man would
give all the substance of his house for love,
it would utterly be contemned.*

Song of Solomon 8:7

*Take my life, and let it be
consecrated, Lord, to thee;
take my moments and my days;
let them flow in ceaseless praise.
Take my hands, and let them move
at the impulse of thy love.
Take my feet, and let them be
swift and beautiful for thee.
Take my love, my Lord, I pour
at thy feet its treasure store.
Take myself, and I will be
ever, only, all for thee.*

–Frances Ridley Havergal

$\mathcal{H}$eavenly Father, it is good to remember that everything that lives and breathes is sacred to you. We must never feel superior to any other human being—for we are all precious in your eyes. You have given us life, and we must make the choices that lead to kindness and peace. You created us, but how we live together is up to us. Thank you.

$\mathcal{F}$ear not, for a mighty shield of love protects you. Doubt not, for mighty wings of faith surround you.

*There is no fear in love; but perfect love
casteth out fear: because fear hath torment.
He that feareth is not made perfect in love.*

1 John 4:18

*T*know you will not fail to lift me up from my
sorrow and gently deposit me upon the shore. And though my
body is tired and my spirit is weary from weeping, I offer
myself to you in complete surrender, so that you may fill my
nets with the bounty of your eternal peace and the comfort of
your infinite love.

*Ask an angel what he has and he will say,
"enough." Ask an angel what he needs and he
will say, "nothing." ask an angel what he knows
and he will say, "only love."*

But love ye your enemies, and do good,
and lend, hoping for nothing again; and
your reward shall be great, and ye shall be
the children of the Highest: for he is kind
unto the unthankful and to the evil.

Luke 6:35

O Lord, your gift of love is often distorted in this world of ours. You are the source of the only perfect love we will ever know. Thank you, Lord, for abiding in us and helping us love ourselves and others. On this day, Lord, I pray that you will draw near to anyone who is feeling unloved. May they accept your unconditional love so they will know what true love is!

Greater love hath no man than this, that
a man lay down his life for his friends.

John 15:13

*L*ord, I know I encounter them every day: your loved ones who are—on their own strength—desperately trying to make some sense out of this life. Help me reach out to them. Give me the words to say and the gentle approach that will lead them to the knowledge of you and to the immense blessings you want to bestow on them.

*L*oneliness can sometimes feel like a thick, heavy fog blocking out the warm sun and blue sky. But remembering that God loves me helps clear away the fog and gives me a new sense of clarity and direction. Even if people cannot find time for me, God is always there, unfailing in his love and steadfast care.

I know that when I am sad, lonely, and afraid, I can turn to God for his loving grace. With mercy and compassion, God hears my cries and comes to my aid, ready to take away my burdens and heal my wounded heart. He gives me wisdom and understanding, and helps me to forgive those who have hurt me. God's unceasing love for me is what grace is all about.

Charity never faileth: but whether there be prophecies, they shall fail; whether there be tongues, they shall cease; whether there be knowledge, it shall vanish away.

1 Corinthians 13:8

*Two souls with but a single thought,
Two hearts that beat as one.*

– Friedrich Halm

How good it is, Almighty One, to bask in the warmth of your love. To know nothing more is required than this: receive your good gifts from above.

Though I walk in the midst of trouble,
thou wilt revive me: thou shalt stretch forth
thine hand against the wrath of mine enemies,
and thy right hand shall save me.

The Lord will perfect that which concerneth
me: thy mercy, O Lord, endureth for ever:
forsake not the works of thine own hands.

Psalm 138:7–8

Lord, your word created all there is. Let it now create a powerful restoration within me. Your love sustains all life. Let it now sustain and renew me. Your strength holds up the galaxies. Let it now hold me up and give me support. Your light reaches the far ends of the universe. Let it shine its healing energy upon me now. Amen.

*S*ave me, O God; for the waters are come in unto my soul.

I sink in deep mire, where there is no standing: I am come into deep waters, where the floods overflow me.

I am weary of my crying: my throat is dried: mine eyes fail while I wait for my God.

Hear me, O Lord; for thy lovingkindness is good: turn unto me according to the multitude of thy tender mercies.

Psalm 69:16

The Lord thy God in the midst of thee is mighty; he will save, he will rejoice over thee with joy; he will rest in his love, he will joy over thee with singing.

Zephaniah 3:17

Encircle me in the arms of your love.
Fill me with your perfect peace.
Though my soul faints,
Sustain me through hope in your word.

So many things will offer themselves to me for "worship" today. But reveal yourself, God, in all your creativity, as the only being worthy of my true adoration.

For I am persuaded, that neither death,
nor life, nor angels, nor principalities, nor pow-
ers, nor things present, nor things to come,
Nor height, nor depth, nor any other creature,
shall be able to separate us from the love of
God, which is in Christ Jesus our Lord.

Romans 8:38–39

From the dark night of the soul
Comes the blessing of the dawn.
From the deep wounds of the heart
Comes the gift of love reborn.
From the chaos of confusion
Comes the calm of clarity.
From the anguish of discord
Comes the peace of harmony.
From the grieving of great loss
Comes the happiness of new life.
From the coldness of despair
Comes the warmth of our Father's light.

Chapter 2

Forgiveness

And be ye kind one to another, tenderhearted, forgiving one another, even as God for Christ's sake hath forgiven you.

Ephesians 4:32

And when ye stand praying, forgive,
if ye have ought against any: that your
Father also which is in heaven may forgive
you your trespasses.

Mark 11:25

God, when things go wrong, we usually blame you first. Forgive us for even considering that you would deliberately hurt one of your very own children. What could you possibly have to gain? Thank you for your presence, and please forgive our many sins.

Father, I need to understand that forgiveness is not dependent on my feelings but rather on a determination of my will. Help me form a few well-chosen words of forgiveness. Amen.

$\mathcal{F}$orgiveness is the central virtue in God's treasure chest—God's forgiveness of us and our forgiveness of others and ourselves. At times we find that forgiveness comes very easily, even for grievous and painful hurts. But many times, we seem powerless to forgive, no matter how hard we try. This is when God's forgiving grace has the opportunity to touch and change us and then be extended to others through our example.

Say not thou,
I will recompense evil;
but wait on the Lord, and he
shall save thee.

Proverbs 20:22

God, I pray for the strength and the wisdom to know what to do in this situation. I pray for enough love to forgive this person for the pain they have caused me and to forgive myself for the ill will I have harbored against this person. Help me be a truly forgiving person so that the weight of resentment may be lifted from my shoulders. Amen.

*And when they were come to the place,
which is called Calvary, there they crucified
him, and the malefactors, one on the right
hand, and the other on the left.*

*Then said Jesus, Father, forgive them; for
they know not what they do. And they
parted his raiment, and cast lots.*

Luke 23:33–34

Heavenly Father, I ask for your healing presence. Protect me from the worldly hurts and evil that have clouded my life and robbed me of joy. Help me forget the past, to let go of grudges, and to make a new start. Take away the darkness of my sorrow, and flood it with the light of your love. Forgive me, so I might forgive others. Amen.

$\mathcal{L}$ord, you have seen each time when I've been abandoned by those in whose love I have trusted. You have known the loneliness in my soul. I must confess to you that it causes me to wonder if your love has failed me, too. I need you to assure me that you are still here and that you will always stay with me.

$\mathcal{H}$eavenly Father, teach me to forgive others their transgressions and to let go of angers and resentments that poison the heart and burden the soul. Teach me to love and understand others and to accept them as they are, not as I wish they would be. Amen.

*I acknowledge my sin unto thee,
and mine iniquity have I not hid. I said, I will
confess my transgressions unto the Lord; and
thou forgavest the iniquity of my sin. Selah.*

*For this shall every one that is godly pray
unto thee in a time when thou mayest be found:
surely in the floods of great waters they shall not
come nigh unto him.*

*Thou art my hiding place; thou shalt preserve
me from trouble; thou shalt compass me about
with songs of deliverance. Selah.*

Psalm 32:5–7

For he shall have judgment without mercy, that hath shewed no mercy; and mercy rejoiceth against judgment.

James 2:13

Dear God, the wound between this person and me seems too deep to heal, and the chasm of misunderstanding seems to wide to leap across. I pray for guidance that I may do my part to close the wound and narrow the gap between us with love, understanding and forgiveness. Amen.

This is not a choice I would make, for me or for the one who went against my standards, my hopes. It's a riddle, O God, why you give us freedom to choose. It can break our hearts. Comfort me as I cope with a choice not mine; forgive any role I had in it. Help me separate doer from deed as I pass on your words to all: "...nothing can separate us." Not even poor choices I sometimes make myself.

So that contrariwise ye ought rather to forgive him, and comfort him, lest perhaps such a one should be swallowed up with overmuch sorrow.

2 Corinthians 2:7

Father, when we stand to cross the metaphorical bridge of forgiveness, please give us a little push to get us going. Amen.

Dear Lord and Father of humankind,
Forgive our foolish ways;
Reclothe us in our rightful mind,
In purer lives Thy service find,
In deeper reverence, praise.

—John Greenleaf Whittier

Judge not, and ye shall not be judged: condemn not, and ye shall not be condemned: forgive, and ye shall be forgiven.

Luke 6:37

Lord, I need you to help me with the concept of forgiving people over and over again for the same behavior. I know you taught that there was no limit to the number of times we should forgive someone, but I get so weary of doing it, Lord. Help me to have a heart of forgiveness, so ready to forgive that I do so before the person who has wronged me even seeks my forgiveness. There's freedom in that kind of forgiveness, Lord. Help me claim it for my own. Amen.

*C*omfort me in my day of need with a love that is infinite and true. Ignore my lack of desire to forgive and forget. Fill my anger with the waters of peace and serenity that I may come to accept this situation and move on to a greater level of understanding and knowing.

*L*ord God, it is hard for us to accept when someone else hurts us. We don't want to talk to the person anymore. We consider our friendship to be over. And all because our pride is bruised. Please help us recognize when we are not giving others a chance. Amen.

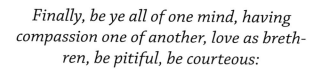

Finally, be ye all of one mind, having compassion one of another, love as brethren, be pitiful, be courteous:

Not rendering evil for evil, or railing for railing: but contrariwise blessing; knowing that ye are thereunto called, that ye should inherit a blessing.

1 Peter 3:8–9

God, I do not intend to hurt you and others. I am not always sure what happens in those times when I do hurt you and others. I am thankful that you forgive. Please help others to forgive me, too. Remind us all to follow your teachings. We pray that you will guide and comfort us.

$\mathcal{L}$ord, what comfort I find in the knowledge that you know everything I've ever done. I know going over my sins with you is still necessary for my growth and development, but it helps to know I'll never have to hear you say, "I can't believe you did that!" You know my strengths and my weaknesses. You know my joy and my shame. And yet you still forgive me and have hope for me. Thank you, Lord, for caring enough to truly know me—and for loving me anyway.

Heavenly Father, give us the forgiving spirit we so badly need to heal the wounds of the past. Help us live "the better life" by making peace with our enemies and understanding that they, too, need your love. Amen.

Lord, sometimes I fall so low that I feel ashamed and unworthy of being in your presence. At these times, remind me that it is never too late to throw myself at your feet and beg for your forgiveness and mercy. You are all good and all powerful, and your love for us never wavers. I can become whole and joyful again through you.

And all things are of God, who hath reconciled us to himself by Jesus Christ, and hath given to us the ministry of reconciliation;

To wit, that God was in Christ, reconciling the world unto himself, not imputing their trespasses unto them; and hath committed unto us the word of reconciliation.

2 Corinthians 5:18–19

I pray, Lord, for the ability to learn forgiveness. Often within my heart there is much that is negative. I pray to learn to let go of those feelings. I pray to learn to forgive others as I wish to be forgiven. I pray for the gifts of understanding and compassion as I strive to be more like you. Amen.

Then came Peter to him, and said, Lord, how oft shall my brother sin against me, and I forgive him? till seven times?

Jesus saith unto him, I say not unto thee, Until seven times: but, Until seventy times seven.

Matthew 18:21–22

Father God, we know that to receive the blessing of healing, the heart must be open. But when we are mad, we close off the heart as if it were a prison. Remind us that a heart that is shut cannot receive understanding, acceptance, and renewal. Even though we feel angry, we must keep the heart's door slightly ajar so your grace can enter and fill our darkness with the light of hope.

If my people, which are called by my name,
shall humble themselves, and pray, and seek
my face, and turn from their wicked ways;
then will I hear from heaven, and will forgive
their sin, and will heal their land.

2 Chronicles 7:14

Lord, it is tempting and easy to cast a scornful eye on those around us and note every fault. When my pride tempts me to do so, prompt me to turn the magnifying glass on myself instead. If I keep in mind how much I need your forgiveness every day, my love for you will never grow cold. I know you are willing to forgive each and every fault if I only ask.

Dear God, help us to see that none of us are immune to losing ourselves or to hurting one another. Please help us stay on course so we may find our own true essences. Amen.

Lord, I confess to you,
sadly, my sin;
all I am, I tell to you,
all I have been.
Purge all my sin away,
wash clean my soul
this day;
Lord, make me clean.
Then all is peace and
light this soul within;
thus shall I walk with you,
loved though unseen.
Leaning on you, my God,
guided along the road,
nothing between!

–Horatius Bonar

*D*ear God, help us start anew. Teach us how to heal by learning new ways to live. Amen.

*D*ear God,

Help my unbelief.

When I'm in pain, I forget that you care about me.

I forget that you have helped me through my trials.

I forget that you hold me in your arms to keep me safe.

I forget that you are feeling my pain with me.

I forget that you love me,

I forget that I am important to you.

Show me your presence—let me feel your enveloping love.

Heal my hurting soul.

Thank you for staying with me even in my unbelief.

Amen.

After this manner therefore pray ye:
Our Father which art in heaven, Hallowed
be thy name.

Thy kingdom come, Thy will be done
in earth, as it is in heaven.

Give us this day our daily bread.

And forgive us our debts, as
we forgive our debtors.

And lead us not into temptation,
but deliver us from evil: For thine is the
kingdom, and the power, and the glory,
for ever. Amen.

Matthew 6:9–13

$\mathcal{L}$ord, why is it that frustration sometimes turns to despair and self-destruction? There are so many destructive forces in the world as it is, why do I sometimes make a bad situation worse because of my bitter or hopeless attitude? How often I wish I could take back thoughtless, hurtful words I have said to a loved one during the course of a trying day. How many times I wish I could have a "do over." But there are no "do overs" in real life. Help me to make amends and handle things better the next time I am challenged.

$\mathcal{W}$hen will the rain let up, Lord? Oh, soon: may your presence be to me as cleansing droplets of mercy, these clouds only filtering in glorious gold and purple the blazing rays of your grace.

Forgive us, Lord, our sins, for failing to live up to your standards of goodness and justice. We confess our shortcomings. Make us willing to change and help us become persons of godly character. Amen.

Deliver me, O God, from a slothful mind, from all lukewarmness, and all dejection of spirit. I know these cannot but deaden my love to you; mercifully free my heart from them, and give me a lively, zealous, active, and cheerful spirit, that I may vigorously perform whatever you command, thankfully suffer whatever you choose for me, and be ever ardent to obey in all things your holy love.

—John Wesley

Lord, help us move beyond the times we hurt one another, the times we willingly misunderstand, the times we cherish our differences, and the times we assume we know all there is to know about each other and turn away. Amen.

*W*hen we learn to forgive the past, we sow the seeds for a glorious future.

*E*ven though we may call ourselves "loving," often we justify an action by saying, "he deserved that." When someone comes against us with evil and we respond with good, we are showing mercy.

*E*ven if we feel we've been wronged by someone, if we soften our hearts and forgive the one who wronged us, the burden of bitterness will be lifted. This change is certain to affect the lives of those around us.

*W*hatever the relationship, forgiveness is a truly healing gift for the people involved. In a marriage, the power of true forgiveness cannot be overstated.

Forgiveness **63**

When on the fragrant sandal-tree
The woodman's axe descends,
And she who bloomed so beauteously
Beneath the keen stroke bends,
E'en on the edge that wrought her death
Dying she breathed her sweetest breath,
As if to token, in her fall,
Peace to her foes, and love to all.
How hardly man this lesson learns,
To smile and bless the hand that spurns;
To see the blow, to feel the pain,
But render only love again!
This spirit not to earth is given—
One had it, but he came from heaven.
Reviled, rejected, and betrayed,
No curse he breathed, no plaint he made,
But when in death's deep pain he sighed
Prayed for his murderers, and died.

—Author Unknown

*For if ye forgive men their trespasses,
your heavenly Father will also forgive you:*

*But if ye forgive not men their
trespasses, neither will your Father forgive
your trespasses.*

Matthew 6:14–15

The strongest friendships have experienced the joy of genuine forgiveness.

God knows that as hard as we may try, there are times when we will make human mistakes. Even so, if we trust in him and ask his forgiveness, He will bless us with mercy and peace.

The story is told that someone asked Martin Luther if he "felt" that he had been forgiven. His reply:

"No, but I'm as sure as there's a God in Heaven. For feelings come, and feelings go, and feelings are deceiving. My warrent is the Word of God, naught else is worth believing."

—Martin Luther

A few well-chosen words of forgiveness are like an antiseptic that cleanses the wound and promotes healing.

*F*irst we are hurt, and feelings of anger may consume us. Then thoughts of how we can get revenge come creeping in. But only when we are ready to relinquish the hurt is there an opportunity for forgiveness and healing to begin.

Bless the Lord, O my soul, and forget
not all his benefits:

Who forgiveth all thine iniquities;
who healeth all thy diseases;

Who redeemeth thy life from
destruction; who crowneth thee with lov-
ingkindness and tender mercies;

Psalm 103:2–4

Forgiveness is not easy. Often it requires us to become far more than we were before; more mature, more accepting, and more compassionate. But once we forgive and stretch ourselves, we can never go back to being that unforgiving and resentful person we were before. We have been opened up, expanded, and set free.

Once we forgive and stretch ourselves, we are opened up, expanded, and set free.

The greatest gift we can offer someone is our forgiveness, for it has the dual power to set the other person free and to set us free as well.

And they shall teach no more every man his neighbour, and every man his brother, saying, Know the Lord: for they shall all know me, from the least of them unto the greatest of them, saith the Lord: for I will forgive their iniquity, and I will remember their sin no more.

Jeremiah 31:34

*G*od prefers that we make an effort, even if we should initially fail. He will eagerly forgive our mistakes in the hope that we will learn and grow from them.

*B*ecause none of us will ever be able to live a perfect life, we need to be understanding and practice forgiveness in our daily lives.

*L*ove and forgiveness walk hand-in-hand. Our relationships with God and others are intertwined in this dynamic.

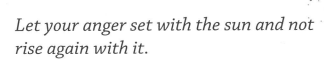

Let your anger set with the sun and not rise again with it.

—*Irish Proverb*

One of the greatest peace-robbers in our lives is anger. It affects our minds, our bodies, and our emotions. If we choose to let go of it, we can embrace peace again.

God pardons like a mother who kisses the offense into everlasting forgetfulness.

—*Henry Ward Beecher*

In thankfulness for present mercy, nothing so becomes us as losing sight of past ills.

—*Lew Wallace*

Chapter 3

Nature

I will speak of the glorious honour of thy majesty, and of thy wondrous works.

Psalm 145:5

*L*ord, I can hear your voice in the bubbling brook, see your beauty in the petals of a flower, and feel your gentle breath in the evening breeze and in the soft kiss of a child. Thank you for all of these gifts.

T remember it—coming from a swim and lying back in white sand—the gift of a moment to rest, to sit in reverie, to watch, to close eyes and think of nothing but the sound of breaking waves. Yes, you were there with the sounds and the sunshine, and I am thankful.

*A*lthough the rain still falls, Creator God, it takes such a little bit of sun to create a rainbow, your sign of promise and presence.

Holy Spirit, the life that gives life.
You are the cause of all movement;
You are the breath of all creatures;
You are the salve that purifies our souls;
You are the ointment that heals our wounds;
You are the fire that warms our hearts;
You are the light that guides our feet.
Let all the world praise you.

—Hildegard of Bingen

The heavens are thine, the earth also is thine: as for the world and the fulness thereof, thou hast founded them.

Psalm 89:11

It's easy to praise you for your majesty and power when we see thundering waterfalls, crashing ocean waves, or majestic sunsets. Help us learn to praise you when we see a dewdrop, a seedling, or an ant.

Lord, bring me to the place where peace flows like a river, where soft green grasses gently hold the weight of my tired body, where the light of a new sunrise casts warmth.

I am grateful, God of Hope, for the gift of each new day, each new season, like the one unfolding around me now in flower and birdsong, in seedling and bud. When they arrive as surely as dawn follows night and bloom follows bulb, I am uplifted by the fulfillment of your promise.

Move our hearts with the calm,
smooth flow of your grace. Let the river of your
love run through our souls. May my soul be
carried by the current of your love, towards the
wide, infinite ocean of heaven. Stretch out my
heart with your strength, as you stretch out the
sky above the earth. Smooth out any wrinkles
of hatred or resentment. Enlarge my soul that it
may know more fully your truth.

—*Gilbert of Hoyland*

I have made the earth, the man
and the beast that are upon the ground,
by my great power and by my outstretched
arm, and have given it unto whom it seemed
meet unto me.

Jeremiah 27:5

Little drops of water,
Little grains of sand,
Make the mighty ocean
And the pleasant land.
Little deeds of kindness,
Little words of love,
Help to make earth happy
Like the heaven above.

–Julia Fletcher Carney

Praised be You, my Lord, through our Sister Mother Earth, who sustains us, governs us, and who produces varied fruits with coloured flowers and herbs. Praised be You, my Lord, through Brother Wind and through the air, cloudy and serene, and every kind of weather. Praised be You, my Lord, through Sister Moon and the stars in heaven: you formed them clear and precious and beautiful. Praised be You, my Lord, through Brother Fire, through whom You light the night and he is beautiful and playful and robust and strong. Praised be You, my Lord, with all your creatures, especially Sir Brother Sun, who is the day and through whom you give us light. And he is beautiful and radiant with great splendours and bears likeness of You, Most High One.

*—St. Francis of Assisi,
"The Canticle of Brother Sun"*

And God called the dry land Earth; and the gathering together of the waters called he Seas: and God saw that it was good.

Genesis 1:10

Like sun that melts the snow,
my soul absorbs the grace
that beats in gentle, healing rays
from some godly place.
Like rain that heals parched earth,
my body drinks the love
that falls in gently, soothing waves
from heaven up above.

Tree or person, lightning can topple whatever it hits. Console us with your truth that trouble, trauma, tragedy—like lightning—just happen. Random and without malice from you. Should it strike, we'll look for rainbows, assured of your presence as we pick up the pieces.

*G*od, I couldn't help noticing all the loveliness you placed in the world today! This morning I witnessed a sunrise that made my heart beat faster. Then, later, I watched a father gently help his child across a busy parking lot; his tenderness was much like yours. While inside a department store, I spied an elderly couple sitting on a bench. I could hear the man cracking jokes; their laughter lifted my spirits. Then early this evening, I walked by a woman tending her flower bed; she took great pleasure in her work, and her garden was breathtaking. Later, I talked with a friend who is helping some needy families; her genuine compassion inspired me. Thank you, Lord, for everything that is beautiful and good in the world.

A friendly voice in the dark of night,
The tentative rays of morning light,
A host of butterflies high in flight,
A rainbow extending far out of sight——
All these miracles tell me this:
Angels really do exist.

Father, make me resilient like the sandy beach upon which the waves crash. Make me strong like the mighty willow tree that bends but does not break in the high winds. Give me the patience and wisdom to know that my suffering will one day turn to a greater understanding of your ways, your works, and your wonders.

Green grass and blossoms blanket the earth,
For spring is the season of renewal and rebirth.
Tender buds, woodland creatures, new life without end——
How much of this do we owe to our many angel friends?

*G*od, you are so great. It is always the right time to worship you, but morning is best. Praise for the dawning light that streams in through this window. Praise for the sound of the birds as they flit through in the air. Praise for the little spider crawling along on the ceiling. Praise for the smell of coffee and the warmth of a cup in my hands. Praise for the flowering plants—and even those weeds growing by the house. Praise for the neighbors walking along the sidewalk and the clouds moving by, too. Most of all, praise for the breath that keeps flowing in and out of my lungs. Yes, this is the greatest item of praise: that you alone are my life—all life itself. Without you, all is dust. Praise . . . for you.

Lord, may I be wakeful at sunrise to begin a new day for you, cheerful at sunset for having done my work for you; thankful at moonrise and under starshine for the beauty of the universe. And may I add what little may be in me to your great world.

—The Abbot of Greve

We thank thee,
O Lord whose finger touched our dust,
O Lord who gave us breath.
We thank thee, Lord, who gave us sight and sense
to see the flower,
 to hear the wind,
 to feel the waters in our hand,
 to sleep with the night and wake with the sun,
 to stand upon this star,
 to sing thy praise,
 to hear thy voice.

$\mathcal{L}$ord, it's so easy for us to get bogged down in the details of life on this earth. But when we have the opportunity to gaze up at the stars on a clear night, it is easy to remember that there is so much more to your creation than our relatively in-significant lives. You placed the stars and know them by name, Lord, and you know us by name too. We are blessed to be even a tiny part of your magnificent creation! That you also care so deeply for us is the best gift of all.

$\mathcal{T}$o see a world in a grain of sand
And a heaven in a wild flower,
Hold infinity in the palm of your hand
And eternity in an hour.

*B*less the soil beneath our feet, the sky overhead, and make us one with it. We are catching on, catching up with ourselves, creator God, and catching a whiff of the garbage we're burying ourselves beneath. Catching, too, a glimpse of the fading streams and trash-strewn seas we have long ignored.

Bless and use our reclamation efforts, for it is a task we can't accomplish alone. With your help, we can bind up and reclaim this poor old earth. We feel whispers of hope in the winds of changed hearts and minds, for we recall your promise to make all things new——even this earth we shall yet learn to tend. We are grateful for another chance.

*S*pirit, carry me like a feather upon the current to a place of serenity. Let the waters flow over me like cleansing balm. Set me upon the dry place, where life begins anew. Spirit, carry me like a feather back home again.

Deep peace of the running waves to you.
Deep peace of the flowing air to you.
Deep peace of the smiling stars to you.
Deep peace of the quiet earth to you.
Deep peace of the watching shepherds to you.
Deep peace of the Son of Peace to you.

—Gaelic Prayer

*But ask now the beasts, and they shall
teach thee; and the fowls of the air, and
they shall tell thee:*

*Or speak to the earth, and it shall teach
thee: and the fishes of the sea shall declare unto thee.*

*Who knoweth not in all these that the
hand of the Lord hath wrought this?*

*In whose hand is the soul of every living
thing, and the breath of all mankind.*

Job 12:7–10

What a relief in this throwaway world of ever-changing values to know that you, O God, are the same yesterday, today, and tomorrow. Your trustworthiness and desire for all your children to have good things never varies. You are as sure as sunrise and sunset.

$\mathcal{W}$e are blessed by your enveloping spirit as near to us as daily changing weather. Your comfort touches us like gentle rain and hushed snow. And, like the sound of thunder and glimpse of searing lightning, you startle us with new opportunities.

$\mathcal{W}$inters can be long, Lord, as I've complained before, and hope elusive. Thank you for sending me outdoors. My spirit soars at the sight of a woodchuck waking from winter sleep. I rub sleep from my eyes, grateful for signposts of change, like pawprints in the mud, leading me to springs of the soul.

Creation shouts to me, Lord, about how amazing you are. I see the wonder of your wisdom in everything from the solar system to how bodies of water feed into one another to the life cycles of all living creatures. Everywhere I turn there is something that makes me think about how creative and insightful you are. Thank you for this universe that speaks without words. I hear it loud and clear, and it tells me of your magnificence.

How beautiful is the work of your hands, Lord! I am grateful for the world of nature. How wonderful it is to see the plants and animals you have created. How awesome is your power on the shape of the Earth! Thank you, Lord, for making the landscape and creating so much beauty in the natural world.

Lord, we praise you for all the beauty and wonder you've placed in the world. How creative of you to think of a creature as exuberant and joyful as the hummingbird! How interesting that you sprinkled spots on the backs of the newborn fawns that follow along behind their mother through our backyard. Let us never become so accustomed to your glorious creation that we take it for granted, Lord. You've blessed us with a wonderland, and we thank you for it.

Thank you, Lord, for the signs of your power. Thank you for the awe I feel during a thunderstorm or at the sight of a monument in nature. Thank you for the thrill I feel when I see one of your works in all its glory. It is good to know your power and feel its presence in my life.

Today, in the dreary days as we head toward winter, I celebrate flowers. How wonderful it is to see their bright colors. I am grateful for the chance to bring flowers into my home to brighten a dreary day. Thank you for the colors and smells of spring and the opportunity to welcome them into my life at any time of year.

Blessings often come to us shaded in disguise.
Miracles work magic veiled from human eyes.
Knowing healing comes from pain,
that every loss makes way for gain,
or that the sun shines after rain,
and what goes round comes back again,
Marks the difference between the ignorant and the wise.

Through strife or storm
or darkest night,
My angel is there to show
me God's light.

*W*ithout seeming rhyme or reason, hope allays the soul's worries with the certainty of hummingbirds, who know precisely the day to fly south.

*L*ike the weather, love has its change of seasons. It begins with the springtime of courtship, merging into the sweet summer of devotion. When autumn arrives, so, too, do the rewards of commitment and sharing. Winter often brings a sense of comfort and contentment, but just as the weather is cyclical, so, too, is love. Just beyond winter is an even brighter spring of renewed passion, internal beauty, and deeper devotion.

If we had no winter, the spring would not be so pleasant.

–Anne Bradstreet

*H*ope melts the frost from the tiniest leaf, allowing it to grow stronger in the healing light of the sun.

*L*iving in harmony with nature's seasons awakens us to spring's renewal, fall's cozy slowness, winter's savory rest, and summer's exuberance. Thus we are reminded to honor each season's energies for the wisdom they hold.

*A*ll around leaves are falling, drifting, swooping in the wind. They become a whirligig, a dance of wind and nature. They are a picture of the heavenly places where lighthearted beings are carried by the invisible power of love.

Rest is not idleness, and to lie sometimes on the grass under trees on a summer's day, listening to the murmur of the water, or watching the clouds float across the sky, is by no means a waste of time.

—Sir John Lubbock

Faith is like a tiny seed of belief inside us that grows into a mighty tree, each leaf a new direction, each branch a new opportunity.

Enjoy all of creation, each leaf and flower and every small pebble along the way. Embrace the hope of each new morning, and the last ray of sunshine to fall at day's end.

*S*cattered by a loving hand,
signs of hope are as close as
crocuses unfurling in the snow.

Beautiful pastel colors,
Pink, blue, golden, white,
Brightening every highway and byway,
Colors soft and light.
Covering the earth in a rosy glow,
A special sunset for all to see.
Brushstrokes of heavenly beauty
On a canvas that spans the seas.
I can't describe my feelings
As I watch him paint the sky,
A sense of solace covers the earth
As another day goes by.

$\mathcal{L}$ike the evergreen, hope never dies, but stands tall and mighty against the coldest winter winds until the summer sun returns to warm its outstretched branches.

Angels help us see beautiful blooms in an overgrown patch of weeds. And when our gardens are thriving, they point toward the loveliness of creation in the fragrance of each blossom.

$\mathcal{W}$hen we struggle in the search for harmony, we need only remember to look for nature for the answer.

I love fishing. I can think of no greater pleasure than to sit alone toward evening by the water and watch a float.

—Anton Chekov

In the solitude of a natural setting, the heart discovers serenity, the soul knows abiding peace, and the spirit finds renewal.

The world acquired a new interest when birds appeared, for the presence of birds at any time is magical in effect. They are magicians that transform every scene; make of every desert a garden of delights.

—Charles C. Abbott

While flowing rivers yield a blameless sport
Shall live the name of Walton: Sage benign!
Whose pen, the mysteries of rod and line
Unfolding, did not fruitlessly exhort.

–William Wordsworth

In the peaceful quiet of a dark night, the moon's beauty catches your eye and captures your soul.

Seated on an outcropping of rock high above the snowbound valley, my eye is drawn to the evergreen, and hope stirs within my breast.

A little garden in which to walk, an immensity in which to dream, at one's feet that which can be cultivated and plunked; overhead that which one can study and meditate upon; some herbs on earth and all the stars in the sky.

—Victor Hugo

*H*opeful eyes look upward, penetrating the thick blanket of clouds to the clear blue skies beyond.

*S*eek comfort in the garden, seek adventure in the wilderness, but seek the truth within yourself.

The heart of the mountain is the wild ravine where these two streams mingle in perpetual coolness and shadow. No path leads to it and few are the feet which have found a way to its beauties. There is a peculiar charm in a spot unknown to the many. Its loneliness endears it to the mind, and gives its associations a rarer flavor.

—Frank Bolles

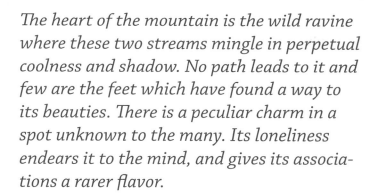

Kindness sows a seed within me that begins to sprout where before all was barren. Leaves of trust start to bud, and I branch out. I take in gentle caring and loving nudging and realize I might just go ahead and bloom! After all, God arranged spring after winter.

Chapter 4

Giving Thanks

In every thing give thanks: for this is the will of God in Christ Jesus concerning you.

1 Thessalonians 5:18

We thank you, God,
for the moments of fulfillment:
the end of a day's work,
the harvest of sugar cane,
the birth of a child,
for in these pauses
we feel the rhythm
of the eternal.

—Hawaiian prayer

Thank you, God, that even when I fret, I know without a doubt that you are using my unique, special gifts and talents to nurture and teach my children. When I get down on myself and am unsure of my abilities, remind me that your commitment to me is lifelong.

$\mathcal{B}$lessed Creator, thank you for the loving people in my life. Thank you for their open hearts and minds. Thank you for making them like you. Amen.

$\mathcal{G}$od, I give thanks for the wisdom you share with me when I am trying to understand my own actions or someone else's. You know what is best, and you have my highest good in mind. I will turn to you for the advice and guidance I need. Thank you, God, for being a strong and loving presence in my life. Amen.

How lonely we are when trouble strikes. Send us a sign, Lord. We long for a message, a hand reaching toward us. And just as God promised, we're visited by a presence in dream and daylight revelations, and we are grateful for God's personal, one-on-one caring.

Lord, you are the light I follow down this long, dark tunnel. You are the voice that whispers, urging me onward when this wall of sorrow seems insurmountable. You are the hand that reaches out and grabs mine when I feel as if I'm sinking in despair. You alone, Lord, are the waters that fill me when I am dried of all hope and faith. I thank you, Lord, for although I may feel like giving up, you have not given up on me. Amen.

And when ye will offer a sacrifice
of thanksgiving unto the Lord, offer it at
your own will.

Leviticus 22:29

God, we thank you for this food
for the hands that planted it
for the hands that tended it
for the hands that harvested it
for the hands that preprared it
for the hands that provided it
and for the hands that served it.
And we pray for those without enough food
in your world and in our land of plenty.

O Lord, we give thanks for your presence, which greets us each day in the guise of a friend, a work of nature, or a story from a stranger. We are reminded through these messengers in our times of deepest need that you are indeed watching over us. Lord, we have known you in the love and care of a friend, who envelops and keeps us company in our despair. When we observe the last morning glory stretching faithfully to receive what warmth is left in the chilly sunshine, we are heartened and inspired to do the same. When we are hesitant to speak up and then read in the newspaper a story of courage and controversy, we find our voice lifted and strengthened by your message in black-and-white type. Lord, we are grateful receivers of all the angelic messages that surround us every day.

Give thanks unto the Lord, call upon his name,
make known his deeds among the people

1 Chronicles 16:8

*G*racious and healing God, thank you for everything you have done for me in the past.

You have restored me in unexpected ways and I will never be the same.

Thank you for being with me in the present and for the bright future you have planned for me. I pray for those who don't know you yet, who don't understand how you bless them again and again.

Use me to share the gratitude I feel, that others may grow to know you and your power.

In the name of Jesus, who healed the sick and made the lame to walk, I pray. Amen.

"Thanks" is the song of angels with their faces turned toward heaven.

*L*ord, help my eyes to see all the ways you are working in this world. Because of your great compassion, because of your active involvement, the effects of everything you accomplish are multiplied many times over. We praise you, Lord, and pray you will continue to be involved in our lives and in our world. And may our deeds and thoughts always honor you.

*B*less those who mentor, model, and cheer me on, Lord, urging me toward goals I set, applauding as I reach them, and nourishing me to try again when I don't. Remind me to be a cheerleader. I plan to say thanks to those who are mine.

No matter the worries I have, small or large, you, O God, are there ahead of me with promises of help and support that relieve me and free me from getting stuck in the mire of my fear. I am grateful.

Count your blessings, name them one by one:
Count your blessings, see what God hath done.
Count your blessings, name them one by one;
Count your many blessings, see what God
hath done.

—Johnson Oatman, Jr.,
"Count Your Blessings"

O Lord, please help me to understand that I won't always get what I pray for. In the same regard, I want to learn to thank you more for everything you do give me. Amen.

$\mathcal{F}$or the promise you unfold with the opening of each day, I thank you, Lord.
For blessings shared along the way, I thank you, Lord.
For the comfort of our home filled with love to keep us warm, I thank you, Lord.
For shelter from the winter storm, I thank you, Lord.
For the gifts of peace and grace you grant the family snug within, I thank you, Lord.
For shielding us from harm and sin, I thank you, Lord.
For the beauty of the snow sparkling in the winter sun, I thank you, Lord.
For the peace when the day is done, I thank you, Lord.

Therefore will I give thanks unto thee,
O Lord, among the heathen, and sing
praises unto thy name.

Psalm 18:49

*D*ear Lord, when I am sad, you give me hope. When I am lost, you offer me direction and guidance. When I am alone, you stand beside me. When my heart aches with sorrow, you bring me new blessings. Thank you for your gifts of grace, of love, and of healing. Amen.

*L*ord God, why is it that we tend to hold so tightly to the things of this world? We know in our hearts that everything we have is ours only by your grace and great generosity. When we accumulate more than we need, it only builds barriers between ourselves and you. Thank you for your provision, Lord. May we learn to hold everything loosely, knowing it is only borrowed.

*W*ake up in the morning and be grateful for the new day ahead. Every 24 hours is an opportunity to live life more fully, and love more deeply. Look at each moment and see the gift it brings. Cherish the present as it unfolds. Then, when you go to sleep at night, be thankful for the experiences God gave you. This is a life well-lived.

*G*od, help me notice the little things and be grateful for them. All too often, we rush through life and don't notice the blessings all around us. I am grateful for the chance to see beauty in the smallest details. Help me remember to slow down and look. I am grateful for the little bits of beauty scattered through my day.

*To the end that my glory may
sing praise to thee, and not be silent.
O Lord my God, I will give thanks unto
thee forever.*

Psalm 30:12

*L*ord, if I were to boil down all the good news in the universe and look to see what I'd ended up with, there would be the eternal realities of your goodness, your love, and your faithfulness. And in this world, I don't have to look far for them—family, food, shelter, clothing, seasons, tides, sun, moon, stars, life, beauty, truth, salvation. And that's just a sampling, a preview of a much longer list. I'm moved to praise you and to tell you how much I love you back.

*L*ord, we stand in awe of your great sacrifice for us. Your journey to the cross is the reason we are free from the destruction of sin. It's why we can be forgiven and be united with you throughout eternity. No sacrifice is too great in response to your love for us. Keep us ever mindful, Lord. Keep us ever grateful.

*L*ord, with each breath I take I am aware that it is you who breathed life into me. My next breath is as dependent on you as my last breath was. And I can confidently rest in the knowledge that it will be you and you alone who will determine when the last breath leaves my body and I go to be with you. Today, Lord, I thank you for the gift of life and for each breath I take.

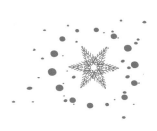

I will give thee thanks in the great congregation:
I will praise thee among much people.

Psalm 35:18

I sit in what once was and grieve what is lost forever. And yet words once heard float like mind-perfume, opening up a floodgate of memory, recalling the moments when those words were spoken. And I am comforted. Thank you, O God, for the gift of remembering.

Dear Lord, thank you for healing my heart and bringing joy and meaning back into my life. Thank you for the people who truly care for me. Help me be a soothing and joyful presence in their lives as well. Amen.

Thank you for your wise ways, Lord. Following them fills my life with true blessings—the riches of love and relationship, joy and provision, peace and protection. I remember reading in your Word that whenever I ask for your wisdom from a faith-filled heart, you will give it, no holds barred. So I'll ask once again today for your insight and understanding as I build, using your blueprints.

You, O Lord, are our refuge. When the days are too full and sleep is hard to come by, we simply need to escape to a quiet place and call on you. In your presence we find strength for our work and peace for our troubled minds. We are grateful for the comfort of your embrace, Lord.

*H*eavenly Father, help us examine every passing day in order to find purpose in our lives. We want our time to be worthwhile. Remind us to count all our blessings, big and small. Amen.

*I will praise the name of God with a song,
and will magnify him with thanksgiving.*

Psalm 69:30

*W*e praise you, Lord, for eternal life. And we thank you for your love for each one of us. Amen.

*T*here's so much to be grateful for in this life! Thank you, God, for your many blessings.

Savior, like a shepherd lead us,
Much we need thy tender care;
In thy pleasant pastures feed us,
For our use thy folds prepare.
Blessed Jesus, blessed Jesus,
Thou hast bought us, thine we are.
Blessed Jesus, blessed Jesus,
Thou hast bought us, thine we are.

—Dorothy A. Thrupp

May we always recall and be thankful
For guiding lights along the way,
For mentors and teachers who shaped us
Into the people we are today.

Without praise, the soul withers.

But I will sacrifice unto thee with the voice of thanksgiving; I will pay that that I have vowed. Salvation is of the Lord.

Jonah 2:9

Lord, I'm looking forward to sharing a home with you. Thank you for becoming poor so that I could become rich. Amen.

Wondrous God, I praise your name.
Your Word is life.
I believe you can heal me.
Be with me when I am sick, and remind me
to praise you when I am well.
Thank you for healing me in the past,
And for future healing.
Keep me in good health
That I might serve you
And praise your name.
Amen.

We plow the fields and scatter
The good seed on the land,
But it is fed and watered
By God's almighty hand;
He sends the snow in winter,
The warmth to swell the grain,
The breezes and the sunshine,
And soft, refreshing rain.
All good gifts around us
Are sent from heaven above:
Then thank the Lord, O thank the Lord
For all His love.

–Matthias Claudius

*G*ive thanks and praise for what you have, and your prayers are already answered.

And he took the cup, and gave thanks, and gave it to them, saying, Drink ye all of it.

Matthew 26:27

Gratitude is an attitude of loving what you have, and this undoubtedly leads to having even more. When you open your eyes to the bountiful blessings already in your life, you realize just how abundant the world really is. Suddenly, you feel more giving, more loving, and more open to even greater blessings. Gratitude is a key that unlocks the door to treasures you already have, and it yields greater treasures yet to be discovered.

I will tell you, I have heard... God has two dwellings, one in heaven and the other in the meek and thankful heart.

—Izaak Walton

Gratitude may be the most highly underestimated virtue. We think of love, hope, faith and the power of prayer and forgiveness. But how often do we stop each day and give thanks for all the blessings in our lives? Are we too focused on what we lack, what we don't have, don't want, don't need? By opening the heart and mind to focus on gratitude, we unleash a treasure of unceasing good that's just waiting to overflow into our lives. A grateful person knows that by giving thanks, they're given even more to be thankful for.

We cannot in any better manner glorify the Lord and Creator of the universe than that in all things, how small soever they appear to our naked eyes, but which have yet received the gift of life and power of increase, we contemplate the display of his omnificence and perfections with utmost admiration.

—Anton Van Leeuwenhoek

*L*ord, your Word is so alive—so vibrant—that it almost seems illuminated when I am reading it. When I am troubled, opening the Bible is like turning on a comforting light in a dark, gloomy room. Thank you, Lord, for loving us so much that you gave us your wisdom to illuminate our lives.

*T*hank you, God, for second chances. Sometimes I feel like I can't do anything right. It's embarrassing to make mistakes. It's embarrassing to show others that I am less than perfect. Thank you for giving me the chance to try again, to make things right, and to improve myself. Help me find the courage to try again and show the world my best qualities!

Now thank we all our God
with hearts and hands and voices,
who wondrous things hath done,
in whom this world rejoices;
who, from our mothers' arms,
hath blessed us on our way
with countless gifts of love,
and still is ours today.

–Martin Rinkart, translated by
Catherine Winkworth

Thanksgiving is nothing if not a glad and reverent
lifting of the heart to God in honour and praise for
His goodness.

–James R. Miller

*B*e thankful for all of creation. Embrace the hope of each new morning and the last ray of sunshine to fall at day's end.

*G*od, living in your grace
empowers me to be
the woman I was born to be!
I look and listen for your
guidance, and I move with
gratitude in the direction
that will help me achieve
the great things you expect
of me.

*T*hank you, Lord, for reaching out and drawing me under
your wings. Even though I am just one of billions of people who
need you, your love is so great that you know my troubles, are
concerned for my welfare, and are working to renew my dreams.
I am so blessed to have you to turn to when I am faced with a
calamity, and I am so very grateful that I have you to lean on. I
praise you with all my heart. Amen.

*T*oday, may I feel grateful for those moments when something heavenly graces my daily routine.

Any one thing in the creation is sufficient to demonstrate a Providence to a humble and grateful mind.

—Epictetus

*T*hank God when the pain ends, when once again we're well and whole and strong. Thank God when our bodies are released from the blinding, mind-numbing hurts that affect our whole lives. Thank God when we have complete victory over pain.

The most important prayer in the world is just two words long: "Thank You."

—Meister Eckhart

*W*ater that runs over moss-covered rocks: This is the sound of praise. Fingers that play upon ivory keys: This is the sound of worship. Silence that speaks even better than words: This is the sound of my thankful heart.

Were there no God, we would be in this glorious world with grateful hearts: and no one to thank.

—Christina Georgina Rossetti

Gratitude makes a lady out of a damsel. It makes a gentleman out of a beggar. It makes the angels seem that much closer.

*G*ratitude lifts us, like angels, above the cares that weigh us to the earth.

Blessed and praised be the Lord, from whom comes all the good that we speak and think and do.

—Teresa of Avila

When I first open my eyes upon the morning meadows and look out upon the beautiful world, I thank God I am alive.

—Ralph Waldo Emerson

Glorious indeed is the world of God around us, but more glorious the world of God within us.

—Henry Wadsworth Longfellow

Thou who has given so much to me, give me one thing more: a grateful heart.

—George Herbert

*C*herish the chance to work and play and think and speak and sing; all simple pleasures are opportunities for grateful praise.

When did you last pause to recognize God's wisdom in the timing of events in your life? Have you thanked Him?

O worship the King, all glorious above, O gratefully sing His power and His love.

—Robert Grant

Chapter 5

Joy

And all the people came up after him, and the people piped with pipes, and rejoiced with great joy, so that the earth rent with the sound of them.

1 Kings 1:40

*In his neck remaineth strength, and
sorrow is turned into joy before him.*

Job 41:22

*Life itself cannot give you joy
unless you really will it.
Life just gives you time and
space—it's up to you to fill it.*

–Chinese Proverb

God, grant me the courage to let go of shame, guilt, and anger. Free me of all negative energies, for only then will I become a conduit for joy and a channel for goodness. Amen.

Take time to work—
It is the price of success.
Take time to think—
It is the source of power.
Take time to play—
It is the secret of perpetual youth.
Take time to read—
It is the fountain of wisdom.
Take time to be friendly—
It is the road to happiness.
Take time to dream—
It is hitching your wagon to a star.
Take time to love and be loved—
It is the privilege of the gods.
Take time to look around—
It is too short a day to be selfish.
Take time to laugh—
It is music to the soul.

—Anonymous

'Tis easy enough to be pleasant,
When life flows along like a song;
But the man worth while
is the one who will smile
When everything goes dead wrong.

—*Ella Wheeler Wilcox*

Father, this morning I woke up, and the gift of life was still within me. What a privilege! I don't want to lose wonder of it for even one day. So help me to live with purpose and joy, not waiting for what today might bring me, but rather looking for opportunities to be and do all that you've created me for. And, most of all, thank you for being with me in each moment, showing me the way of abundant living.

Thou wilt shew me the path of life: in thy presence is fullness of joy; at thy right hand there are pleasures for evermore.

Psalm 16:11

God, shine your healing light down upon me today, for my path is filled with painful obstacles and my suffering fogs my vision. Clear the challenges from the road I must walk upon, or at least walk with me as I confront them. With you, I know I can endure anything. With you, I know I can make it through to the other side, where joy awaits. Amen.

Dear God, we trust you to show us joy when the time comes. We know that good follows bad. Please help us be patient. Amen.

When we think of joy, we often think of things that are new—a new day, a new baby, a new love, a new beginning, the promise of a new home with God in heaven. Rejoicing in these things originates with having joy in the God who makes all things new. Rather than relying on earthly pleasures to provide happiness, the Scriptures command that we rejoice in God and in each new day He brings. Joy is a celebration of the heart that goes beyond circumstances to the very foundation of joy—the knowledge that we are loved by God.

And my soul shall be joyful in the Lord: it shall rejoice in his salvation.

Psalm 35:9

*B*lessed are you who know how to celebrate the goodness of life. Blessed because you choose to see the grace above and beyond the pain. Blessed because you see a potential friend in every stranger you meet. Blessed because you know the darkest clouds have brilliant silver linings. And most blessed because: All you ever knew of the half-empty glass was that it was almost full.

*D*ear God, help us work to live instead of living just to work. Lead us to the green pastures where we can enjoy the companionship of our loved ones and the pleasures that restore us. Amen.

Whatever is right and pure,
excellent and gracious,
admirable and beautiful,
fill my mind with these things.
Too much of the world
comes to me in tones of gray and brown.
Too great the temptation
to indulge obsessive thoughts and sordid plans.
Guard my mind; place a fence around my motives.
The pure, the lovely, the good—Yes!
Only those today.

Enliven my imagination,
God of new life, so that I can
see through today's troubles
to coming newness. Surround
me with your caring so that
I can live as if the new has
already begun.

God with me lying down,
God with me rising up,
God with me in each ray of light
Nor I a ray of joy without Him,
Nor one ray without Him.

Christ with me sleeping,
Christ with me waking,
Christ with me watching,
Every day and night,
Each day and night.
God with me protecting,
The Lord with me directing,
The Spirit with me strengthening,
For ever and for evermore,
Ever and evermore,
Amen.

—Celtic Prayer

*Pleasant thoughts are sent your
way with a heartfelt wish
for a happy day.*

wish to extend my
love, Lord. So give me hands
quick to work on behalf of the
weak. Cause my feet to move
swiftly in aid of the needy.
Let my mouth speak words of
encouragement and new life.
And give my heart an ever-
deepening joy through it all.

*Hope is the joyful liberation of the heart from
the darkest prison of despair.*

*Then will I go unto the altar of God, unto
God my exceeding joy: yea, upon the harp
will I praise thee, O god my God.*

Psalm 43:4

Give us eyes with which to see, noses with which to sniff, ears with which to hear the faintest sound along the paths you have set for us, O God of Daily Joys. Following you is a whole experience——body, mind, and soul.

*Today, I long to make a difference——to pass
along peace and joy and somehow resurrect
hope in weary hearts.*

$\mathcal{J}$oy grows in the most unlikely of places. It reaches up in the middle of poverty to dance in the eye of a child at play. It spreads itself across the face of an old man whose rheumatism, while all too present, is forgotten the moment he greets an old friend. Joy wedges itself through the cracks of loneliness when the voice at the other end of the phone line is that of someone familiar and loved. How is it that joy is found where it is least expected? It is, no doubt, because true joy roots itself not in the shifting sands of circumstance but in the rich soil of a grateful heart.

How blessed are the good memories, Lord! In fact, I am beginning to see that my happiness can consist largely in the looking back. For that I am thankful, as I lay here, unable for the moment to be active.

Thank you for the funny bone, Lord, placed next to hearts broken by anxiety and fear. A good belly laugh is a gift from you, expanding and healing heart, lungs, and mind.

Lord, I do believe! And because of my hope of life with you in eternity, there is all the more meaning for life today. There's meaning in my choices, my relationships, my work, my play, my worship. It all matters, it all counts, and I live knowing one day I'll stand in your presence with great joy.

Cultures throughout the world have used dance to express joy. Dancing is done at feasts, at weddings, and at almost every other celebration. In fact, God's word commands us to dance as an expression of worship and joy.

When we experience true joy, we will naturally express it. As God pours joy into our lives, we can bring it back to Him.

If you truly open your heart
To new opportunities,
You will see
That the possibilities
Are endless.
So look to your future
With the excitement and joy
It truly deserves.

With an eye made quiet by the power of
harmony and the deep power of joy, we
see into the lives of things.

–William Wordsworth

Angels skip along the seashore picking up shells,
kissing each one, and whispering, "Good job!"
Angels traipse through the galaxy, touching
stars and dancing on planets. Angels waltz
through the heavens, full of joy and worship,
flowing with majesty, rhythm, and love.

And young and old come out to play
On a sunshine holiday.

–John Milton

The real joys in life are those that
cannot be calculated by any known unit
of measurement.

When you smile, dear friend, I feel joy
in my heart.

"On with the dance, let the joy be unconfined!" is my motto, whether there's any dance to dance or any joy to unconfine.

−Mark Twain

There's a fulfilling joy that comes from serving other people rather than putting our own desires first.

There's a place of renewal and happiness within you. All you need to do to reach it is withdraw your attention from the outside world and focus on the strength and the energy inside yourself.

When I think of God, my heart is so full of joy that the notes leap and dance as they leave my pen: and since God has given me a cheerful heart, I serve him with a cheerful spirit.

—Franz Joseph Haydn

It is wonderful to watch an uninhibited person express joy. We long to give our souls permission to rejoice so freely.

Fill the cup of happiness for others, and there will be enough overflowing to fill yours to the brim.

—Rose Pastor Stokes

When my mind's highest meditations meet and join in jubilant dance, inspiration greets me with a lighted path.

Restore unto me the joy of thy salvation;
and uphold me with thy free spirit.

Psalm 51:12

How you feel is determined by how you think you feel. If you think you're happy you will be; if you expect good things to happen they will.

To live happily is an inward power of the soul.

—Marcus Aurelius

Go where the energy makes your heart palpitate and your spirit sing, for there you will find fulfillment.

Love divine, all loves excelling,
joy of heav'n to earth come down,
fix in us thy humble dwelling,
all thy faithful mercies crown.
Jesus, thou art all compassion,
pure, unbounded love thou art;
visit us with thy salvation,
enter ev'ry trembling heart.
Breathe, O breathe thy loving spirit
into ev'ry troubled breast;
let us all in thee inherit,
let us find thy promised rest.
Take away our bent to sinning,
Alpha and Omega be;
end of faith, as its beginning,
set our hearts at liberty.
Finish then thy new creation,
pure and spotless let us be;
let us see thy great salvation,
perfectly retsored in thee.
Changed from glory into glory,
till in heav'n we take our place,
till we cast our crowns before thee,
lost in wonder, love, and praise!

–Charles Wesley

*Sometimes I demand,
"God give me joy!"
and nothing happens.
Yet joy flows naturally,
lavishly,
when I seek to
know Him,
love Him, and
serve Him.*

There are joys which long to be ours. God sends ten thousand truths, which come about us like birds seeking inlet; but we are shut up to them, and so they bring us nothing, but sit and sing a while upon the roof and then fly away.

—Henry Ward Beecher, Life Thoughts

Happiness is contageous! If allowed to spread, it can infect the whole universe with joy.

Make a joyful noise unto the Lord,
all the earth: make a loud noise,
and rejoice, and sing praise.

Psalm 98:4

Remember, in the first place, that the Vine was the Eastern symbol of Joy. It was its fruit that made glad the heart of man. Yet, however innocent that gladness—for the expressed juice of the grape was the common drink at every peasant's board—the gladness was only a gross and passing thing. This was not true happiness, and the vine of the Palestine vineyards was not the true vine. "Christ was the true Vine." Here, then, is the ultimate source of Joy. Through whatever media it reaches us, all true Joy and Gladness find their source in Christ.

–Henry Drummond

O spread the tidings 'round, wherever man is found,
wherever human hearts and human woes abound;
let every Christian tongue proclaim the joyful sound:
The Comforter has come!
The Comforter has come, the Comforter has come!
The Holy Ghost from heaven,
the Father's promise given;
O spread the tidings 'round, wherever man is found—
the Comforter has come!
The long, long night is past, the morning breaks at last,
and hushed the dreadful wail and fury of the blast,
as over the golden hills the day advances fast!
The Comforter has come!

—Frank Bottome

May you be poor in misfortune, rich in
blessings, slow to make enemies, quick to
make friends. But rich or poor, quick or
slow, may you know nothing but happiness from this day forward.

—Traditional Irish Blessing

*They that sow in tears shall
reap in joy.*

Psalm 126:5

Help us to relax, Lord of calming seas, so that we don't become numb to the joy and awe of children, of family. For it's socially acceptable to kick off our shoes and tangibly feel the love. Make us alive, O God, to the holy grounds of life, and save us from taking these special places for granted.

Father, instill in me the gifts of humor and joy. Teach me how to lift downcast spirits and dispense the medicine of good cheer in your name.

*T*oday I am thankful for the gift of laughter. How wonderful it is to let out a big belly laugh and feel joy rush through my entire body! Thank you for the people who make me laugh, whether it is a neighbor or friend or a performer on television. Thank you for allowing me to experience joy bursting out of me, and help me make others feel happy with my laughter as well.

You have the power to make happiness a way of life instead of an occasional experience.

Joy is energy to an angel. God's joy sends them on their way. Our own joy keeps them dancing in the wind.

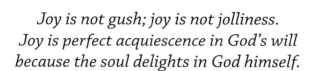

Joy is not gush; joy is not jolliness.
Joy is perfect acquiescence in God's will
because the soul delights in God himself.

–H. W. Webb-Peploe

We all want to be happy, but joy goes much deeper. Joy is not based on circumstances or feelings, which change like the weather. True joy comes from a celebration of the heart over the things that do not change—things that come from God.

We miss so much joy just because we don't open ourselves up to all there is to enjoy. We can choose to embrace all the joy that today has to bring.

For ye shall go out with joy,
and be led forth with peace: the mountains
and the hills shall break forth before you
into singing, and all the trees in the field
shall clap their hands.

Isaiah 55:12

Each sunrise reveals a new opportunity to
experience joy.

Mirth is the sweet wine of human life.
It should be offered, sparkling with
zestful life, unto God.

–Henry Ward Beecher

Chapter 6

Faith

Thy mercy, O Lord, is in the heavens;
and thy faithfulness reacheth unto
the clouds.

Psalm 36:5

*I will sing of the mercies of the Lord for ever:
with my mouth will I make known thy faithfulness to all generations.*

Psalm 89:1

*Lord, perfect for me what is lacking of thy
gifts; of faith, help thou mine unbelief; of
hope, establish my trembling hope; of love,
kindle its smoking flax.*

–Lancelot Andrewes

*Even though I walk through the darkest val-
ley, I fear no evil; for you are with me; your
rod and your staff—they comfort me.*

*Y*ou call me to courage, Lord, but incrementally, as a child emboldened to walk along placing each small foot in larger footprints. Following Father or Mother—as I am following you—knowing a path marked out this way—just step by step—but you can only lead to safety.

Lord, since you exist, we exist. Since you are beautiful, we are beautiful. Since you are good, we are good. By our existence we honour you. By our beauty we glorify you. By our goodness we love you.

—Edmund of Abingdon

*Mine eyes shall be upon the faithful
of the land, that they may dwell with me:
he that walketh in a perfect way,
he shall serve me.*

Psalm 101:6

I am feeling my way in this darkness, God, and it seems I'm going in circles. Yet you have reminded me—quietly, just now—that encircled by your love with every move in any direction I go no closer to you—nor farther either—than already centered I am.

Grant, O Lord, that we may live in thy fear, die in thy favour, rest in thy peace, rise in thy power, reign in thy glory.

It's hard, Lord, to reveal my heart to you, though it's the thing I most want to do. Remind me in this dialogue that you already know what is within me. You wait——O thank you——hoping for the gift of my willingness to acknowledge the good you already see and the bad you've long forgotten.

Lord, you are here,
Lord, you are there.
You are wherever we go.
Lord, you guide us,
Lord, you protect us.
You are wherever we go.
Lord, we need you,
Lord, we trust you,
You are wherever we go.
Lord, we love you,
Lord, we praise you,
You are wherever we go.

In silence I kneel in your presence——bow my heart to your wisdom; lift my hands for your mercy. And open my soul to the great gift: I am already held in your arms.

Lord, if we could see the future, it would be easy to have hope. Real hope is when we can't see the end of the road, but still trust you to lead us there.

As storm clouds gathered, Father, I used to run for cover, panicked and picking a favorite escape. None of them worked for long, Dear God, and none of them k ept me safe. No more running then. I see it clearly now: Wherever I am standing is a special place, under the shadow of your sheltering wing.

Thy faithfulness is unto all generations: thou hast established the earth, and it abideth.

Psalm 119:90

*L*ord, when I turn to you and trust you, you are very glad. Make me glad, too, as I learn to share your joy in finding what you lost. Amen.

*L*ord, I come to you boldly and gladly. Accept me as your child, and meet my needs. Amen.

*D*ear Lord, help me to build on a firm foundation by relying on your wisdom, diligently seeking your direction in all I do, learning to walk in your paths of kindness, peace, and justice to my fellow-man. In Jesus' name, Amen.

As the cold of snow in the time of harvest, so is a faithful messenger to them that send him: for he refresheth the soul of his masters.

Proverbs 25:13

Be thou my vision, O Lord of my heart;
Naught be all else to me, save that thou art:
Thou my best thought, by day and by night,
Walking or sleeping, thy presence my light.
Riches I heed not, or man's empty praise,
Thou mine inheritance, now and always:
Thou and thou only, first in my heart,
High King of heaven, my treasure thou art.

—"Be Thou My Vision"

*A*h, what solace there is in your promise of peace. True help and real peace are to be found from trusting in your guidance and inspiration.

*M*y trust is in you, God of miracles and surprises, for daily I feel your presence in a dozen ways.

*L*ord, help me not accuse you of being untrue when I don't get from you everything I want, for you have promised to meet all my needs. And when I learn to love you supremely and trust you wholly, my desires will find fulfillment in you.

Tend us, loving Creator, and shelter us in the palm of Your hand.

O God, giver of all good things, our faith in you is like a treasure to be mined—it sustains, it inspires, and it provides us with unimagined contentment.

God answers sharp and sudden on some prayers.
And thrusts the thing we have prayed for in our face,
A gauntlet with a gift in't.

—Elizabeth Barrett Browning

*L*ord, I pray I can find a place within my heart where I can let go of worries. I want to be filled with the calmness of a faith in you. Amen.

When life's winds toss me
upon the waves of uncertainty and doubt,
And when the tempest beats me
and rocks of guilt and self-pity,
When my pitiful heart yearns
for love I cannot find,
When the darkness seems darker
and the night longer,
Some unseen hand reaches down,
and with a strength and tenderness
I cannot comprehend,
Pulls me back into the light.

God, I hear your call to action, and I am ready to do your
mighty will in all areas of my life, and in the world. Guide
and direct my path as I step out in faith.

*L*ord, open my eyes that I might see
A whole new level of reality.
When I feel surrounded by my problems
Show me your angelic army surrounding them.
Thank you for the tenacious way they guard me,
Keeping me from potential harm I may never know about.
Let me join my voice with theirs
In praising you, the holy one, the worthy one,
the hallelujah victor over all in heaven and earth.
Glory to you in the highest, Lord.
And peace in my little world.
Amen

*I am weak, but
thou art mighty;
hold me with thy
powerful hand.*

—*William Williams*

*L*ord, far too often we try to steer the course of our lives without consulting you, and we always run into problems. Set us on a true course that will bring us closer to you. Amen.

Lord, you are my lighthouse,
shining like a beacon
in a raging storm,
guiding my way
through the fog and rough seas.

I set my course on you
with patience, perseverance,
and faith, trusting
that you will help me
reach calmer shores.

And when he saw their faith, he said unto him, Man, thy sins are forgiven thee.

Luke 5:20

Dear Heavenly Father, life is full of surprises. Of course, we welcome the good, but when the bad befalls us, we seek reasons for it. It is often in these bad circumstances that we realize how significant and meaningful our faith is. As a result, we pray that you will teach us to always reach out to you. Amen.

God, it's so hard to see your will in suffering. But while I can't understand your ways, I trust your heart. And so I cling to the faith that has sustained me through so many heartaches before, knowing that although it may be all I have, it's also all I need. Amen.

Faith is not merely praying
Upon our knees at night;
Faith is not merely straying
Through darkness into light;
Faith is not merely waiting
For glory that may be.
Faith is the brave endeavor,
The splendid enterprise,
The strength to serve, whatever
Conditions may arise.

—Anonymous

Heavenly Spirit, I long to be healed from my affliction, but I trust your will, your timing, and your plan for my life. I know that you will never give me more than I can handle and that you will always be there to help me. For this I am eternally grateful. Amen.

*F*ather, there are many events in our lives over which we have no control. However, we do have a choice either to endure trying times or to give up. Remind us that the secret of survival is remembering that our hope is in your fairness, goodness, and justice. When we put our trust in you who cannot fail us, we can remain faithful. Our trust and faithfulness produce the endurance that sees us through the tough times we all face in this life. Please help us to remember. Amen.

And his name through faith in his name hath made this man strong, whom ye see and know: yea, the faith which is by him hath given him this perfect soundness in the presence of you all.

Acts 3:16

*L*ord, help me to depend on you to be my source of goodness. I don't always feel like being patient, kind, loving, or joyful, but you are all of these things by your very nature. So right now I place my strengths and weaknesses into your hands, asking you to infuse them with yourself and to make them instruments of good that will serve others for your sake.

God's might to direct me.
God's power to protect me.
God's wisdom for my learning.
God's eye for my discerning.
God's ear for my hearing.
God's word for my clearing.

—St. Patrick

Dear Father God, you sent your son to us to be our Lord, to watch over us, to bring us comfort, strength, hope, and healing when our hearts are broken and our lives seem shattered. We will never be alone, not when you are here with us always and forever. Remind us to look to you for strength. Amen.

*L*ord, how it must amuse you at times to see us orchestrating the details of our days as if everything and everyone were in our control. It's only when you are involved in our plans that things go smoothly, Lord. Teach us to trust that your way is the better way, even when we can't see how every detail will turn out. Our insight is only as good as our reliance on you. Please be with us each day, Lord.

*S*ome days the race feels like a sprint, Lord, and on other days, a marathon. I want to press on, but I need you to infuse my spirit with your strength and steadfastness. I want to run and finish well. Thank you for beginning the work of faith in my life and for promising not to stop working until my faith is complete.

For therein is the righteousness of God revealed from faith to faith: as it is written, the just shall live by faith.

Romans 1:17

*L*ord, maybe it's in the times we aren't sure that you are hearing our prayers that we learn to trust you the most. Eventually—in your time—we hear your answer. We know that you are still sovereign, and all our hopes and dreams are safe in your hands. Even when the answer to a prayer is "no," we are comforted by the knowledge that you care about us and respond to our concerns in a way that will ultimately be for our good.

$\mathcal{L}$ord, this is one of those days when I really don't know which way to turn. I've lost my sense of direction and feel as if I'm sitting on a rock in the forest, wondering which trail will take me back to familiar ground. Lead me, Lord. Send the signs I need to follow to get where you want me to go. I put my trust in you.

$\mathcal{F}$ather, your Word makes it clear to me that the life of faith is not passive. While we wait for you to answer prayer, grant wisdom, and open doors, we also keep our minds sharp and our hearts strengthened by reading and studying your Word, by meeting with you in prayer, and by finding encouragement among other believers. These are the disciplines our souls need to stay focused on ever-present hope.

Imagine having someone always beside you to help you navigate the choppy waters of life? Imagine being able to turn within and ask for strength, courage, love, care, or guidance whenever it is needed? The thing is, you do have someone exactly like this, even though you may have forgotten. You have God.

God, I ask for a bold and courageous faith to get me through these trials and tribulations. Let me stand on my own feet, but steady my footing with the knowledge of your presence. Give me the strength of will to never give up, no matter how crazy life gets.

*L*ord, today I want to praise you for giving me the faith to believe, for faith itself is a gift from you. I lift up to you today all those I know who are having trouble accepting your gift of salvation. Be patient with them, Lord. Reveal yourself to them in a way that will reach them, and draw them into relationship with you. Our lives are incomplete without you, Lord. Send your grace to those who are struggling.

*L*ord, we understand that there are and will be problems in our lives, but please remind us of your presence when the problems seem insurmountable. We want to believe that you know best. We hope to remain patient as we search for purpose. Amen.

Lord, speak to me, that I may speak
In living echoes of thy tone;
As thou hast sought so let me seek
Thy erring children lost and lone.
O teach me, Lord, that I may teach
The precious things thou dost impart;
And wing my words, that they may reach
The hidden depths of many a heart.
O fill me with thy fullness, Lord,
Until my very heart o'erflow
In kindling thought and glowing word,
Thy love to tell, thy praise to show.

—Frances R. Havergal

*O*ur worries are hard to dismiss, Lord. They seem to grow bigger and bigger until they take over our lives. Please help us conquer them, one at a time. Your reassurance is welcome. Amen.

God.
God is.
God is holy.
God is personal and close.
God is there; God is here.
God is spirit.
God is.
God.

God, I hold fast to you at this present moment, for it is the only way for me to have perspective and hope for life beyond this pain I have. And yet, come quickly for I am tired. Fill me with your strength for I feel weak. Add meaning to these days of pain, and finally call me to a new day when I can serve you with a renewed purpose and passion. Amen.

*T*In the midst of mourning life's troubles, you come to us.
In the darkness, your spirit moves, spreading light like a shower of stars against a stormy night sky.

*G*od of All Comfort, I know that with you by my side I am never alone. Your perfect love casts out all fear, doubt, and uncertainty. Your presence emboldens and empowers me. You are the light that leads me to safety again. Amen.

*F*ather God, in you I find comfort and peace after a day of working hard and pushing forward to reach my goals. In you I find strength when I've done all I can do on my own. In you I find my spirit renewed. Amen.

*I*f I put my hope in people, I am often disappointed.

If I put my hope in circumstances, I am often let down.

But when I put my hope in God, I am always taken care of.

God is my rock and my hope, in him is a firm foundation from which I live my life. I may not always get all my hoped-for prayers answered the way I expect, but I get them answered the way God wants me to.

*L*ord God, I am about to throw in the towel! I can't go on without your strength to get me over the edge and into the light again. Help me remember why I chose these goals and dreams to begin with, God. Keep me strong to the finish!

Angels find us, not only when we need them most, but even when we think we are fine on our own.

I stoop
Into a dark tremendous sea of cloud,
It is but for a time: I press God's lamp
Close to my breast: its splendour, soon or late,
Will pierce the gloom: I shall emerge one day.

—Robert Browning

Time is tight, Lord, and I wonder why I bother to pray. The question is answer enough: I need a relationship where I don't have to bluff and hurry. And when I pray boldly? I offer myself as a possible answer to prayer. No time to waste.

Take comfort in God's steadfast presence.
Even when you suffer, take comfort
in the hope of God's healing.
Even when you fear, take comfort
in the hope of God's strength.
No matter what you face, take comfort
in knowing you never walk alone.

My times are in Thy hand;
My God, I wish them there;
My life, my friends, my soul I leave
Entirely to Thy care.

—William F. Lloyd

Though long the weary way we tread,
And sorrow crown each lingering year,
No path we shun, no darkness dead,
Our hearts still whispering, thou art near!

— Oliver Wendell Holmes

*L*ord, I know you will show your goodness and faithfulness to me if I just diligently seek you. The problem isn't your willingness to give, but my tendency to try to do everything by myself rather than leaning on and trusting in you. This silly inclination brings me needless stress and wastes precious time. Today I endeavor to lay my needs and troubles at your feet the minute I begin to feel the least bit overwhelmed.

*W*hen life goes awry, Lord, I need someone to blame so I point the finger at you. Heaven help me, I want it both ways: you as sender and fixer of trouble. Help me know you don't will trouble, for what could you possibly gain? And when the good you want for me isn't possible in the randomness of life, I know you are with me.

When life seems dark and empty
and there's no hope in sight,
look for God to send an angel
to guide you toward the light.

*L*ord, we've tossed our prayers aloft, and hopefully, expectantly, we wait for your answers. As we do, we will: listen, for you speak in the voice of nature; see you as a companion in the face and hand of a friend; feel you as a sweet-smelling rain, a river breeze; believe you can provide encouragement, direction, and guidance for those who have only to ask. We feel your presence.

O may thy spirit guide my feet
In ways of righteousness;
Make every path of duty straight,
And plain before my face.
Amen.

—Joachim Neander

Chapter 7

Growth

But grow in grace, and in the knowledge of our Lord and Savior Jesus Christ. To him be glory both now and for ever. Amen.

2 Peter 3:18

*G*od, I know that you close some doors in my life in order to open new ones. I know that things change and come to an end in order to leave room for new beginnings. Help me have the boldness and enthusiasm to let go of the old and accept the new. Amen.

Change is never easy, but the blessings it bestows upon us are magnificent. Just ask the caterpillar struggling within the tight confines of a cocoon. Even as it struggles, it is becoming something glorious, something beautiful, soon to emerge as a winged butterfly. Change may bring temporary pain and discomfort, but it also brings the promise of a new life filled with joy and freedom and the ability to soar even higher than we ever did before.

But the word of God grew
and multiplied.

Acts 12:24

Lord, speak to me through these pages.
Let me hear your gentle words
Come whispering through the ages
And thundering through the world.

Challenge me and change me,
comfort me and calm me.
Completely rearrange me,
Soothe me with a psalm.

Teach me how to please you,
Show me how to live.
Inspire me to praise you
For all the love you give.

For I know the thoughts that I think toward you, said the Lord, thoughts of peace, and not of evil, to give you an expected end.

Jeremiah 29:11

Our closest friends challenge us to change, to grow, to become the best we can be.

There is in your grace, God of second chances, insufficient evidence to prove my latest setback is a failure. Even if it is, with you, failure is never final but an opportunity to learn and grow. When I goof, as I am prone to do, help me from doubling the problem by failing to take advantage of your redemption.

$\mathcal{O}$ God, you have called each of us to special tasks, purposes, and vocations, equipping us with the skills and energy to perform them. For some, our vocations send us into the labor force; for some, it is soon bringing retirement. For some, it is in full-time homemaking. For some, our vocations are in artistic skills; for some, in volunteering, helping, neighboring. Always, there is that first call from you, God of vision, working through our work to help, heal, change a needful world.

The aim of life is self-development. To realize one's nature perfectly—that is what each of us is here for.

–Oscar Wilde

Who is as the wise man?
And who knoweth the interpretation of a thing?
A man's wisdom maketh his face to shine, and the
boldness of his face shall be changed.

Ecclesiastes 8:1

We don't receive wisdom; we must discover it for ourselves after a journey that no one can take for us or spare us.

–Marcel Proust

Remember the past, and learn from its mistakes.
Honor the present, and make each moment count.
Dream the future, and work hard to make the dream
come true.

Build in yourself a noble character,
morning, noon, and night.

Create in me a clean heart, O God; and renew a right spirit within me.

Psalm 51:10

When the winds of life blow,
I'll hang onto myself.
When the road forks in two,
I'll be true to myself.
When the going gets rough,
I'll have faith in myself.
When the journey gets long,
I'll believe in myself.

Unless you try to do something
beyond what you have already
mastered, you will never grow.

–Ralph Waldo Emerson

I have been asked many times how I have succeeded in this thing or in that thing. In almost every case I have replied that it has required constant, hard, conscientious work. I consider that there is no permanent success possible without hard and severe effort, coupled with the highest and most praiseworthy aims. Luck, as I have experienced it, is only another name for hard work. Almost any individual can succeed in legitimate enterprise that he sets his heart upon, if he is willing to pay the price, but the price, in most cases, is being willing to toil when others are resting, being willing to work when others are sleeping, being willing to put forth the severest effort when there is no one to see or applaud. It is comparatively easy to find people who are willing to work when the world is looking on and ready to give applause, but very hard to find those who are willing to work in the corner or at midnight, when there is no watchful eye or anyone to give applause.

–Booker T. Washington

Sometimes you have to get lost to find your true direction.

The mind is like a garden of fertile soil into which the seeds of our thoughts, ideas, and intentions are planted. With loving care and nurturing attention, those seeds bloom forth to manifest in our lives as wonderful opportunities and events. Those seeds that we choose to either ignore or neglect will simply die off. Thus, our mind constantly turns over old growth into new. It is where we focus our energy and give our love that breaks through the dark soil into the light of day. It then becomes the visible good in our life, casting off new seeds to one day bloom forth in a cycle of renewal and abundance.

The strongest principle of growth lies in the human choice.

–George Eliot

Tossing leaves onto a fire, we name them as regrets and failures from which we choose to be free. We trust you to redeem even these, our deadest moments. They, like autumn leaves, can make the brightest blaze.

Stir new possibilities into life from the embers; fan the sparks of dreams so that we may become one with your purpose for us. It is the root from which we, leaf and human life, begin and from which the most amazing new creation can burst into being, a flame in the darkness.

Today I need your help, God, feeling the need for a breath of fresh air. The old habits and attitudes I've clung to for so long seem stale and worn out. Renew me from the inside out, starting now!

Making progress doesn't always mean continuing forward on the same path. It may mean retracing your steps, taking an unexpected turn, or even stopping to rest and renew your spirit.

One changes from day to day... every few years one becomes a new being.

—George Sand

You heard my prayers to ease my pell-mell race through life, and I am changing. Only you could teach this old dog new tricks. I feel your companionship in walks and exercise, in contemplation and prayer. I'm enjoying this new pace you set.

We know, Lord, that action is the proper fruit of knowledge and all spiritual insight. But so often we wish only to think and muse, without ever doing good toward anyone.

Yes, it's easier to know the good than to do it. It's more comforting to be right than to do the right thing. It's more convenient to sit on the sidelines and give advice than it is to enter the game. It takes less energy to tell others how to carry their burdens than to take up a share of the load with them. But we need to be shaken out of our lethargy, God. We need to recognize that our lack of love is evident in our lack of good deeds. We need to see ourselves, so often, just as we are: sometimes selfish, often lazy.

Change us, God! Open our eyes that we may see the needs around us. Show us the poor—and all the ways we can help. Bring us to the sick—giving us words of comfort and

creative means of succor. Let us no longer pass by the hungry stranger, but move us to offer what is in our hand and in our cupboard to share.

Help us to take the more difficult route of service. Help us to forsake the ease and comfort of a purposeless life. Help us to make friends with the unlikable, to bond with those who are different. Help us to take all we know and put it into every resource at hand, so that action may result for the good of all.

For if you will show us that we, too, are poor and hungry, feeble and needy in so many ways, then we will recognize that our giving can only spring from what we have already been given.

Find the light that makes you shine and then use those rays to illuminate your way.

Make the mistakes of yesterday your lessons for today.

—Theodore Roosevelt

*L*ord, today my heart goes out to all those whose past mistakes weigh them down and make any vision they have of their future dreary at best. Oh, that they might know you and the saving grace you bring! Draw near to them today, Lord. Reveal yourself to them in a way that will reach them, and through your mercy and forgiveness, bestow upon them a new vision—a new hope.

Be always at war with your vices,
at peace with your neighbors,
and let each new year find you a better man.

—Benjamin Franklin

For which cause we faint not;
but though our outward man perish, yet the
inward man is renewed day by day.

For our light affliction, which is but for a moment,
worketh for us a far more exceeding and eternal
weight of glory;

While we look not at the things which are seen,
but at the things which are not seen: for the things
which are seen are temporal; but the things which
are not seen are eternal.

2 Corinthians 4:16–18

*L*ord, so often we find ourselves asking you to save us from bad situations only to discover you quietly revealing to us that we are our own worst enemies! Teach us to break destructive habits and to stop polluting our minds with negative thoughts, Lord. Save us from our enemies, even when it means you have to step in and save us from ourselves!

Dear Lord, I need renewal in my life.
But tell me what you want me to be, first,
then tell me what you want me to do.
Speak, for I am listening,
Guide, for I am willing to follow.
Be silent, for I am willing to rest in your love.

Ambition feeds the spirit just as food feeds the body, energizing the mind to think of better solutions, nourishing the soul to try just one more time, and empowering the heart to reach a little further.

Hopeful people have a peace about them, a way of looking at everything that happens as an opportunity for growth and happiness. Their lives are not any easier than anyone else's; it's their attitude that sets them apart.

And Samuel grew, and the Lord was with him, and did let none of his words fall to the ground.

1 Samuel 3:19

Learning in old age is like writing on sand; learning in youth is like engraving on stone.

–Ibn Gabirol

God, I ask in prayer that you help me hold the vision of a better world, and that I may clearly know my role in making that better world a reality. Let my vision join that of others, to create a more joyful world for those who come after us. Amen.

Lord, thank you for being a God of new beginnings. Give me a fresh start today as I trust in you. Amen.

Lord of the loving heart,
May mine be loving, too.
Lord of the gentle hands,
May mine be gentle, too.
Lord of the willing feet,
May mine be willing, too.
So may I grow more like thee
In all I say and do.

—Author Unknown

This week, give me the wisdom to see
my own imperfections clearly and the
strength to transform them for the better.

Do not look back and agonize over roads not
taken, dreams not pursued. Instead, look ahead
to the future to new roads to discover and new
dreams to fulfill.

Lord,
I like the part about "new" and "better,"
But what's that going to look like? Feel like?
What's all this going to mean?
I want transformation,
But the change part scares me.
Give me strength, Lord.
Help me accept your gift of new life.
Lead me forward.
I put my trust in you.
Amen.

*L*ord, sometimes I get frustrated, especially when I have to face something new. Thank you for giving me an open heart. Help me accept change and rejoice in new experiences and new people. Help me to be grateful for new opportunities and always see the good things even when I am afraid to try something new.

*T*oday I want to spend time with you, Renewing Spirit.
In fact, I'd like to spend the whole day just being in your presence.
For this one day I will not worry about the work I
have to do or the goals I want to accomplish.
I will pull back and simply listen for your guidance.
I'm willing to change my life in order to fit your perfect will,
and I ask that you begin that work in my heart, even now.
I'll let go of personal ambition, for now.
I'll loosen my grip on the things I've wanted to
accomplish and the recognition I've craved for so long.
All of this I give over to you.
I'm content to be a servant for now, quiet and
unnoticed, if that is what you desire.
I'm even willing to be misunderstood, if you will only
respond to my sincere prayer for a renewed heart.
Thank you. I need you so much.

So here I am, waiting. I have answered your call to pray. I have heard your guidance—to sit tight. I have chosen quiet and rest because that is your will for me now. I am sitting on the sidelines, watching the hectic pace around me. I am finding contentment in the little blessings that flow into my days. I am trying to see all these things as big blessings because they come from you. But when can I get going again? When will I do the great works I've envisioned? When will the situation require dedicated action once again? When will I hear the trumpet call? When will I finally move onward and upward? I'm ready Great Spirit! Here I am . . . waiting.

A wise mind knows that adverse events are blessed opportunities for growth in disguise.

As every man hath received the gift, even so minister the same one to another, as good stewards of the manifold grace of God.

1 Peter 4:10

Any dream you can dream,
Any plan you can create,
Is possible.
So begin.

When we awaken the sleeping lion of potential within, we allow it to spring forth in our lives with a mighty, joyful roar.

I will not let the pessimists of the world squelch my belief that what I do can make a difference. I am determined to maintain my inspiration to change the world in whatever small ways I can.

*If you keep taking steps that move you forward,
you will always be heading in the right direction.*

In this time of change, help me to be patient, God.
Let me not run ahead of you and your plans.
Give me courage to do only what is before me and to keep my focus on my responsibilities.
I am tempted to daydream about the future; however, the future is in your hands.
Thus, may I be close to you in all my thoughts, accomplish the task before me today, and do it with all my heart.

Today I am inspired to go beyond the boundaries of my weaknesses, to challenge the walls of my limitations, and believe in endless possibilities.

Father, it stings when the ones I love correct me. I don't like to be wrong or feel like I'm being criticized. But that's just wounded pride revealing itself. Deep down I appreciate learning the truth so I can learn and grow. Flattery feels nice in the moment, but it doesn't do much real good. People who risk hurting me because they love me are the ones I should listen to. Help me get over my wounded pride quickly and move on in light of what I've learned. And bless those who care enough for me to speak the truth in love.

Today belongs to you. It's a clean page you can cover with wonderful, creative images and words that will fill every moment with satisfaction.

*S*pirit of God, keep teaching me the ways of change and growth.
Like the wind, you cannot be tracked or traced.
The breezes blow where they will: silently, invisibly, with great power.
Just as you are working in lives even now.
Let me know your calling as you move in me!
Yes, whisk with your persistent prompting through all the windows of my soul, the dark corners of my heart.

O Lord, let me not live to be useless.

—John Wesley

Lord, teach me to emulate Your goodness.

*L*ord, help us not to be stubborn. We want our broken hearts to heal. Amen.

---

*G*od, give me the insight to discern your will for me. Help me to ignore those who may not have my best interests at heart. Give me strength to stay on my own path until I achieve my goals.

Teach me, teach me, dearest Jesus
In thine own sweet loving, way,
All the lessons of perfection
I must practice day by day.
Teach me meekness, dearest Jesus,
Of Thine own the counterpart;
Not in words and actions only,
But the meekness of the heart.
Teach, Humility, sweet Jesus
To this poor, proud heart of mine,
Which yet wishes, O my Jesus,
To be modeled after Thine.

—*Reverend F. X. Lasance*

Lord, make me an instrument of your peace;
where there is hatred, let me sow love;
where there is injury, pardon;
where there is doubt, faith;
where there is despair, hope;
where there is darkness, light;
and where there is sadness, joy.
Divine Master, grant that I may not so much seek
to be consoled as to console;
to be understood as to understand;
to be loved as to love.
For it is in giving that we receive,
it is in pardoning that we are pardoned,
and it is in dying that we are born to eternal life.

—St. Francis of Assisi

God Almighty, please help me to put everything into perspective. I want to be realistic but also optimistic. Please send me hope and give me strength of mind to make things right again. Amen.

Open up my heavy heart,
That surely day by day,
The bitterness and wrath in me
Will slowly drain away.
God let your spirit enter in
And fill each empty space
With peace and healing to my soul
Through your unending grace.

Your changes touch my life with hope and mystery. God of love and power, I come today ready and eager to experience your power working through me.

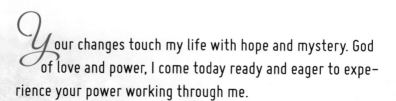

When I'm bored, remind me:
This is the excitement of life—
darkness alternating with light,
down dancing with up,
and inactivity being absolutely essential
—as prelude—to the most fulfilling
experiences of all.

*P*rotect us all and keep us safe,
Help us find our way.
Show us light and make us wise,
Keep the wolves at bay.
Help us not put our trust in doors and locks
and shrill alarms,
Help us rest in angels' strong and everpresent arms.

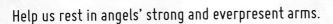

*T*hank you, God, for the wisdom to know when to speak, what to say, and how to say it. Guard my mouth today from any form of foolishness, that in all circumstances I might honor you with my words.

Chapter 8

Family

And will be a father unto you, and ye shall be my sons and daughters, saith the Lord Almighty.

2 Corinthians 6:18

Be kind to your little children, Lord.
Be a gentle teacher, patient with our
weakness and stupidity.
And give us the strength and discernment to
do what you tell us,
and so grow in your likeness.
May we all live in the peace that
comes from you.
May we journey towards your city,
sailing through the waters of sin
untouched by the waves,
borne serenely along by the Holy Spirit.
Night and day may we give you praise
and thanks, because you have
shown us that all things belong to you,
and all blessings are gifts from you.
To you, the essence of wisdom, the foundation
of truth, be glory for evermore.

—Clement of Alexandria

And thy seed shall be as the dust of the earth, and thou shalt spread abroad to the west, and to the east, and to the north, and to the south: and in thee and in thy seed shall all the families of the earth be blessed.

Genesis 28:14

There is a choice, O God, when I spot the crayon markings on the wall, the spilled food, the wet towel on the bed. I have equal breath to scream or laugh. I feel the insistent tickle of my funny bone, and I know which choice you will. Join us as we laugh our way into a better mood.

Thank you, God of inspiration, for the times when you guide me to take my place as an example and a model for my children. For you call us to be loving, tender, and kind. Remind me that this call is more than just creating a family, for the family is Christianity in miniature.

If one perfect day was created by me,
These are the things I would most want to see:
Sun in the morning and moonbeams at night,
Birds singing sweetly, then fluttering from sight,
The whispering wind as it passes my face,
The fragrance of baking so sweet to the taste,
Blossoming flowers with shimmering dew,
The sound of the brook as the water roars through,
A kiss from the people that love me the most,
Tender embraces that snuggle me close,
Smiles from kind strangers just walking by,
The sound of a new born babe's gurgles and sighs,
Proud eyes of a grandmother walking with grace,
An old man with memories that show in his face,
My angel that watches and guards from above,
The laughter of children and, mostly, their love.

For God so loved the world, that he gave his only begotten son, that whosoever believeth in him should not perish, but have everlasting life. For God sent not his son into the world to condemn the world; but that the world through him might be saved.

John 3:16–17

Let me not turn away from the oppressed, the needy, Lord, in order to "protect" the children. Instead, nudge me to enlist them with the invitation to help find solutions that we can do as a family. In this way they learn that they, too, can make a difference.

Dear God, thank you for children who teach us to be open and forgiving. Help us forgive those who hurt us so the pain will not be passed on through the generations. Thank you for forgiving our sins and help us be at peace with our families. Amen.

Sharing has to be one of life's most difficult lessons—for the kids, for me, for everyone, O Bountiful God. Remind me that to choose to "give away" my time, my energy, myself, makes a gracious gift instead of a grudging duty.

Heavenly Father, we are thankful for family. Please bring our family together in happiness. Help us see everything as your children do: with wonder and awe. Glorious are your creations! Thank you for creating us. We love our family. We love you. Amen.

Lord, look down upon my family with merciful eyes, and help us to heal the divides that threaten to grow between us. Guide us toward the solutions that will empower everyone involved, and remind us that we work better when we work together. Help us to speak honestly with each other. Amen.

The most valuable treasure
is the small, simple pleasure
of spending time with family.
Amidst laughter and tears,
we are bound through the years
by a loyalty that never ends.

Sisters are like flowers grown in the same soil;
each has identical roots but offers a unique
beauty to the garden.

As a child, you followed behind your mother and
copied her every move.
As a teenager, you raced in front of her because
you knew all the answers.
As an adult, you walk beside her because she is
your friend.

The warmth of a genuine hug can
send the spirit soaring.

But Jesus called them unto him, and said, Suffer little children come unto me, and forbid them not: for of such is the kingdom of God.

Luke 18:16

Every child born into the world is a new thought of God, an ever fresh and radiant possibility.

–Kate Douglas Wiggin

Those earliest recollections can be fuzzy, but impressions clear as snapshots come easily into focus: the lap where you always felt secure; the shoulder where you snuggled for comfort; the hand that clasped yours and guided you into the world.

A lullaby is simply a parent's love set to music.

If you ask the most accomplished people in the world what is most important to them, they will all give the same answer: family. The love and devotion of family serves as the foundation upon which dreams are built. The support of family acts as wings, which each member can use to fly to new heights of achievement. The honesty and trustworthiness of family creates a sanctuary that can be depended upon in times of struggle and discouragement. The blessings of family bolster the spirit. The pride of family enthuses the heart. With a loving family standing behind you, it becomes much easier to stand on your own.

Where we love is home,
Home that our feet may leave,
but not our hearts.

—Oliver Wendell Holmes

May you know the joy of giving in this family.
Not only on birthdays and holidays, but every
day. Not only when others are looking, but when
no one will ever find out. Give, and give again!
For this is the only true route to happiness, the
only road to lasting peace.

Someday I hope to do for you what you've al-
ways done for me. I'll be the one you turn to for
help, the shoulder you cry on, the confidante
with whom you share your secrets. My dream is
to take care of you the way you've always taken
care of me.

Train up a child in the way he should go: and when he is old, he will not depart from it.

Proverbs 22:6

I am your child.
Your vision created me.
Your dream manifested itself in me.
Your hope molded me.
Your love breathed life into me.

*L*ike the monsters that rioted under my bed, the bad that lurks in the world is always quieted by your presence.

When you were small, you taught me how to live in the moment. I'd ask you, "What's your favorite time of year?" and you'd think for a moment and answer, "This one." That's a pretty wonderful way to live life.

*B*less this gathering of what, at first glance, looks like mismatched parts, encircling God, for we want to become a family. Guide us as we step closer to one another, but not so close as to crowd. Heal wounds from past events that made this union possible.

Bless the children with the courage to try new relatives, new traditions, new homes. Empower them in their anger, helping them know that it is okay and that tears are healing. Assure them that they have the strength to live in two worlds and hearts big enough to love others. Make us, the step-adults, worthy of this love, for it comes at great cost. Help us respect previous traditions and loves and not step too close in our need to belong. For even in the midst of celebrating, there is mourning.

Remind us to take baby steps as we become all you have in mind. Your presence will be our companion, your love our protection, and your wisdom our guidance in this awesome responsibility. Step closer, loving God, and lead us.

Look to grandmas for
a little extra help,
a little extra nudge,
a little more advice,
and a lot of extra love.

Moms always see the best in you,
No matter what you say or do.

And the mother gave, in tears and pain,
The flowers she most did love;
She knew she should find them all again
In the fields of light above.

—Henry Wadsworth Longfellow

*F*ather God, thank you for those angelic persons who bring healing. We will try to mimic their ways.

What a joyful noise is the sound of children playing! Thank you for the chance to play with my children, to be silly with them, and to enter their world and share their zest for life. Thank you for allowing me to be young again as I share their joy and their imagination. Thank you for the gift of having a child's joy.

Thank you, God, that even when I fret, I know without a doubt that you are using my unique, special gifts and talents to nurture and teach my children. When I get down on myself and am unsure of my abilities, remind me that your commitment to me is lifelong.

Aim high, believing that God has great things in store for us as mothers and for our families. Never mind naysayers and "practical" roadblocks, for we are guided by God.

Though we may not choose our family members we eventually come to the understanding that someone far wiser chose them for us. Each family member has something special to teach us, whether it be forgiveness, tolerance, or acceptance. Some members give us nothing but love. Some give us nothing but grief. It is the former we often embrace, yet it is the latter from which we have the most to learn.

Instead of feeling overwrought with demands to the point of being overwhelmed, feel the overflowing joy that comes from daily life in the midst of a hustling, bustling family. The two halves make one marvelous whole of God's balance.

A happy home and family is the source of the greatest human happiness.

As you rush headlong through life, thinking always of making the next leap or rounding the next bend, Mother urges you to slow down.
It's not that she isn't eager for you to get where you're going, she just doesn't want to see you miss anything along the way.

Mothers delight in seeing something of themselves in their daughters. A greater joy, however, comes from glimpsing someone completely new and fascinating.

More than boards and mortar, O God our shelter, this home stands on you as the foundation, giving all who live here a refuge not only for the body but also for the mind and the soul.

The just man walketh in his integrity: his children are blessed after him.

Proverbs 20:7

No man can possibly know what life means, what the world means, until he has a child and loves it. And then the whole universe changes and nothing will ever again seem exactly as it seemed before.

–Lafcadio Hearn

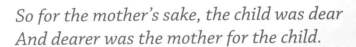

So for the mother's sake, the child was dear And dearer was the mother for the child.

–Samuel Taylor Coleridge

Thank you for long talks and even longer hugs.

Lord, behold our family here assembled. We thank you this place in which we dwell, for the love that unites us, for the peace accorded us this day, for the hope with which we expect the morrow; for the health, the work, the food and the bright skies that make our lives delightful; for our friends in all parts of the earth. Amen.

–Robert Louis Stevenson

A family's love is as sure as the taste of an orange, as certain as the flow of water toward the sea, as familiar as the fragrance of a rose even after the bloom has faded, and as steadfast as the warmth of the sun.

Our families suffer, too, O God, as illness runs its course. Faces show strain from trying not to worry; voices sound too bright from unshed tears. Strengthen them for the grueling task that awaits; their support is life-sustaining.

Bless our homes, dear God, that we cherish the daily bread before there is none, discover each other before we leave on our separate ways, and enjoy each other for what we are, while we have time to do so.

—A Prayer from Hawaii (adapted)

When we are missing an important ingredient in the recipe, we sometimes substitute something that will work for the ideal. Remind us, O Lord, that when it comes to nourishing our family ties, there is no substitute for genuine sharing and caring.

Like potpourri, the unique individual "ingredients" of a family make a wondrous mixture, stirred as it is by God's enduring hand of possibilities.

Dear God, from whom every family receives its true name, I pray for all the members of my family; for those who are growing up, that they may increase in wisdom and love; for those facing changes, that they may meet them with hope; for those who are weak, that they may find strength; for those with heavy burdens, that they may carry them lightly; for those who are old and frail, that they may grow in faith.

—Anonymous

Keep us connected, O God of all time, to those who've come before. Inspire us to tell family tales and to pull out family albums and family Bibles and handed-down antiques to show the connecting links of which your love forges us into a whole.

Honour thy father and thy mother: that thy days may be long upon the land which the Lord thy God giveth thee.

Exodus 20:12

Bless my family, Lord. They are a gift from you, evidence of your unwillingness for me to be alone. Until I see you face to face, may the faces of those I love be to me as your own.

Source of all life and love, let this family be a place of warmth on a cold night, a friendly haven for the lonely stranger, a small sanctuary of peace in the midst of swirling activity. Above all, let its members seek to reflect the kindness of your own heart, day by day.

*W*hat a blessing, Almighty One, to be able to earn a living for the family! To be free of worry about what they will eat, or what they will wear, or where they will sleep. You have given us so much: house, flowers, table and chairs, even a video camera to help us remember these days that are flying by so quickly. Yes, you have given. And your gifts are a serious calling: Show us how to give in return!

Toss a handful of leaves onto a fire, naming them as hope-filled prayers for the children who too soon will be as scattered as the beautiful swirling leaves, and know God follows each.

*If the sun refused to rise,
my love would fill your days with light.
And if the moon forgot its place,
my love would guide you through each night.*

Your family may be less than ideal, but they are your family. It was more than luck or biology that brought you together, and you'll need more than these to keep you together. Faith and forgiveness, kindness and cooperation, laughter and love— these will preserve the precious bonds between you.

Enter and bless this family, Lord, so that its circle will be where quarrels are made up and relationships mature, where failures are forgiven and new direction found.

Children of the same family, the same blood, with the same first associations and habits, have some means of enjoyment in their power, which no subsequent connections can supply.

—*Jane Austen,* Mansfield Park

It is good, dear God, to be a part of this family: circle of love, place of rest, bastion of peace. When every other source of comfort fails, this is where I return. Thank you for being in our midst.

Bless mother and father, sister and brother, grandpa and grandma, uncle and aunt, and all the cousins. Here we are in your sight, this family: May we please you, day by day.

May you find joy and satisfaction in your family life: in building a home and setting up a residence—be blessed! in finding a job and working diligently—be blessed! in taking care of little ones and making friends in the neighborhood—be blessed! in seeking God for all your help and guidance, bringing every care to him, yes, I pray, may you indeed be blessed.

The life of a family centers not on its members but on the love and support that fill the spaces between them.

For all the times I thought I couldn't and you told me I could: Thank you.

My son, hear the instruction of thy father, and forsake not the law of thy mother.

Proverbs 1:8

Parents lend children their experience and a vicarious memory; children endow their parents with a vicarious immortality.

–George Santayana

As I watched the seasons change, I saw each falling leaf, every crystal snowflake, every budding blossom with new amazement...for I watched it all through your wondrous eyes.

Beat upon mine, little heart! beat! beat!
Beat upon mine! you are mine, my sweet!
All mine from your pretty blue eyes to your
feet, my sweet!

—Alfred, Lord Tennyson

You give me a million reasons to glow with pride.

Progress, in the folds of a family, O
God, is not a straight, flat line but
rather ups and downs. Like squiggles on
a heart monitor, they merely chart the
daily rhythm of life. Give me energy and
patience to go with the flow.

Never fear what the world may bring. Its gifts will
far outweigh its troubles. How do I know? Because it
brought me you.

How to weather life: Share your sunny disposition, your bright smile, and your breezy welcome with everyone you meet.

~~~~~~~~~~~~~~

Love children especially, for like the angels they too are sinless, and they live to soften and purify our hearts, and as it were, to guide us.

—Feodor Dostoevsky

*E*nter and bless this family, Lord, so that its circle will be where quarrels are made up and relationships mature; where failures are forgiven and new directions found.

But if any provide not for his own, and specially for those of his own house, he hath denied the faith, and is worse than an infidel.

1 Timothy 5:8

Life in common among people who love each other is the ideal happiness.

—George Sand

*B*less all that happens here, O God, planner and builder. May we find laughter and love and strength and sanctuary. Bless all who visit our love-built home, family and companions with whom we can grow. May we, like you, offer shelter and welcome.

To be alone and in pain is so much worse than being surrounded by friends and family who care.

A happy family is but an earlier heaven.

—Sir John Bowring

Just as the first bird to discover the feeder is full sings out so others can also dine, so can sharing discoveries in a family nourish the whole.

Your mother remembers times when you were almost perfect, as well as times when you were anything but, and she loves you all the more for both.

Guide me, O God, to savor today and all that is yet to be discovered at the hands of my children. I know that what came before and what is yet to be form a marvelous mosaic of the whole.

$\mathcal{G}$uide me, O God, as I encourage the children to be positive—to see the good in each day——each person in their classrooms, new friends, each challenge. Hope and optimism are gifts from your hand that can guide them for life.

Bless us in this time of play together. Let each child know he or she is loved. And let us parents recognize that the love we offer here is the same affection you have already worked in our own hearts.

Visiting with family is like rereading favorite books. Though you know the stories by heart, you are compelled to turn the pages again and again, reliving the precious memories one more time.

The life of a family centers not on its members but on the love and support that fill the spaces in between.

Take a solemn family vow to work for freedoms, large and small. And be wise, kind, and brave in the doing.

A mother doesn't desire gratitude. Your success and happiness are thanks enough.

Taking part in family traditions is such a joyous experience! Today I will take time to recall the traditions I experienced as a child and the family times I shared with those around me. I am grateful for those memories and for the opportunity to share those traditions with my family and friends today. Continuing a tradition feels like taking joyful steps along a path from the past to the future.

*W*e come today, O God, as near strangers gathered from scattered lives, for families no longer live close by. Be the common thread running through our reuniting as we recall and rededicate our ancestors' memory.

Bless us, Lord of history, the next generation, as we take our place as the ancestors-to-be. Bless and guide the young ones, our descendants. Help us be worthy of their remembering.

Through this meal and catching up, embrace us and send us back to our distant homes renewed, refreshed, and revitalized until we once again join hands with you around the family table.

*Y*ou're saintly in your understanding. In one conversation with you, I can dump all my worries and concerns, and you simply carry them away with your angel wings.

Creating a family is like a building coming to life on graph paper, line by line, wall by wall, space by space. In the construction, make sure there are doors that swing both ways.

Thanks for being there during the good times—parties and birthdays and special occasions. Thank you even more for being there in the bad times. What would I do without you?

God setteth the solitary in families: he bringeth out those which are bound with chains: but the rebellious dwell in a dry land.

Psalm 68:6

What's love like? It's like this: Being loved will make you feel light enough to fly up and out into the world. Loving someone will help you find your way home again.

I don't always remember to tell you how much I appreciate you, but I promise that I think of it all the time.

Chapter 9

Friendship

A friend loveth at all times, and a brother is born for adversity.

Proverbs 17:17

Knowing he needs encouragement,
I pray for my friend, Lord.
Lifting my heart to you on his
behalf, may I not fail, either, to
reach my hand to his—just as you
are holding mine.

Companion, confidante, buddy, and pal,
perpetual miracle sent from above.
I thank God each day for the gift of an
angel, beautiful blessing of friendship and love.

Lord, I often pray for others when I need to pray with
others. Show me the power of shared prayer as I meet with
others in your name and in your presence. Amen.

And Elijah said unto Elisha, Tarry here,
I pray thee; for the Lord hath sent me to
Bethel. And Elisha said unto him, As the
Lord liveth, and as thy soul liveth, I will not
leave thee. So they went down to Bethel.

2 Kings 2:2

If life has introduced you to even one person you
can call a true friend, you are truly blessed.

*D*ear God, your love embraces me like the warmth of
the sun, and I am filled with light. Your hope enfolds me in
arms so strong, I lack for nothing. Your grace fills me with
the strength I need to move through this day. For these gifts
you give me, of eternal love, eternal peace, and most of all,
for eternal friendship, I thank you God.

A friend says things to make you feel smart.
A good friend makes you feel strong.
A great friend tells when you do things right.
A best friend tells you when you're wrong.

The world's greatest treasure is the small, simple plea-sure of spending our time with good friends. Amidst laughter and tears we are bound through the years by a loyalty that never ends.

A good friend makes you feel like the brightest star in the sky, the boldest color in a rainbow, the sweetest flower in a garden. She finds the best in you and brings it out for everyone else to see.

And as ye would that men should do to you,
do ye also to them likewise.

Luke 6:31

*D*ear God, shine through me and help me lighten another's darkness by showing the same friendship that you extended. Show me a person that is in desperate need of a friend today. Help me to be sensitive, caring, and willing to go out of my way to meet this person's need right now, whether it be emotional, physical, or spiritual. Thank you that when I need a friend, you are the friend that sticketh closer than a brother. In Jesus' name, Amen.

Having a friend who believes in you is like owning a
second pair of wings. Their faith adds to your own,
creating a jet stream of support that carries you
farther toward the achievement of your dreams.

A friend is one who understands
Any loss or gain.
A friend is one who knows your thoughts,
And whose feelings will remain.
A friend is one who encourages you,
And supports all your decisions,
A friend is one who yearns with you,
And can see your grandest visions.
A friend is one who helps you through,
Those long and stressful days.
A friend is one who lifts you up,
In a hundred different ways.
A friend is one who loves you much,
Just the way you are.
A friend is one who's in your heart,
Whether near to you or far.

A man that hath friends must shew himself friendly: and there is a friend that sticketh closer than a brother.

Proverbs 18:24

What is a good friend, but a column to lean on when times are tough?
What is a good friend, but a shoulder to cry on when things are really rough?
What is a good friend, but a cheerleader to celebrate your success?
What is a good friend, but a confidante who's seen your worst and best?
What is a good friend, but a counselor to support you in hours of strife?
What is a good friend, but a traveling mate on this road we call life?

Father, you help us to live gracefully by blessing us with wonderful friends. Thank you for making them as good as you are. Amen.

Lord, you know better than I know myself that I am growing older, and will some day be old....

Release me from craving to straighten out everybody's affairs.... With my vast store of wisdom it seems a pity not to use it all, but you know that I want a few friends at the end.

....seal my lips on my own aches and pains—they are increasing, and my love of rehearsing this is becoming sweeter as the years go by....

Keep me reasonably sweet. I do not want to be a saint—some of them are so hard to live with—but a sour old woman is one of the crowning works of the devil.

—Anonymous

He that walketh with wise men shall
be wise: but a companion of fools shall
be destroyed.

Proverbs 13:20

God, help me to accept the help I need and to give up my stubborn need to control the outcome of every situation. Show me that sometimes my will is not always the best and that sometimes you send us healing angels in the form of other humans. Thank you. Amen.

May we see those who work among us
for who they truly are:
Angels without wings,
Blessing our lives with the most extraordinary things.

Celebrate friendships that have endured over the years, and remember the hugs, tears, and laughter that sustain them.

Faithful are the wounds of a friend; but the kisses of an enemy are deceitful.

Proverbs 27:6

Thank God for my friends,
who accept the bad with the good.
Together we soar much higher
than I alone ever could.

My friend and I have had a falling-out, Lord. The atmosphere is strained between us; the air is chilly. I don't know what I've said or done to cause this breach in our relationship. I only know we're both at odds. Relieve the anguish that I feel, Lord. Show me how to break the silence. Help me take the first step to mend this rift between us, then you can do the rest. Heal us with your love.

Too often we lie
when people say,
How are you?
We say, "I'm fine."
We smile, and put
on our happy face.

Why can't we be honest,
at least with loved ones,
and say, "I hurt"?
Why can't we cry honest tears
and let a friend
comfort us for a moment—
embrace us
with loving arms,
as we take off
the mask we wear
to hide the pain?

Two are better than one; because they have a
good reward for their labour.
For if they fall, the one will lift up his fellow:
but woe to him that is alone when he falleth;
for he hath not another to help him up.

Ecclesiastes 4:9–10

Does everyone have an angel?
I'd like to believe it's true.
But if ever there's a shortage,
I'd gladly share mine with you.

I awoke this morning with devout thanks-
giving for my friends, the old and the new.

–Ralph Waldo Emerson

The love of a friend has often seemed like my life
preserver, keeping me afloat in turbulent waters.

I wish to be of service, Lord.
So give me courage to
put my own hope and despair,
my own doubt and fear
at the disposal of others.
For how could I ever help without
first being, simply . . . real?

When I am weak and stumble, you give me
sympathy instead of sermons. You show me
mercy instead of meanness. You speak tender-
ly instead of tearing down my already-fragile
ego. You are a true friend.

True friendship is a knot that angel hands
have tied.

—Anonymous

Heavenly Father, I am glad to have even just one companion, but you have sent me many more! I thank you for my friends
and family. I am happy to have so many shoulders on which I can
lean. Amen.

*T*hank you for the healing power of friends and for the positive emotions friendship brings. Thank you for sending companions to me so we can support and encourage one another and share our joys and sorrows. My friends represent for me your presence and friendship here on earth. Please keep them in your care, Father. We need each other, and we need you. Amen.

We cannot tell the precise moment when friendship is formed. As in filling a vessel drop by drop, there is at last a drop which makes it run over; so in a series of kindnesses there is at last one which makes the heart run over.

—Samuel Johnson

True wealth cannot be measured in material objects or wordly possessions, but in the depth and quality of our friendships.

This is my commandment,
That ye love one another, as I have loved you.
Greater love hath no man than this, that a man
lay down his life for his friends.
Ye are my friends, if ye do whatsoever
I command you.
Henceforth I call you not servants;
for the servant knoweth not what his lord doeth:
but I have called you friends; for all things that I
have heard of my Father I have made
known unto you.

John 15:12–15

A healthy friendship enhances our lives. What a blessing to have someone who wants to share all our joys and sorrows. We should continually strive to be the kind of friend God would like us to be—and the kind of friend that we would like to have.

Come walk with me
through life, my friend,
arm in arm we'll stroll.
With love and hope
to light our path,
and faith to guide our souls

It's easy to love a friend for all the things we have in common. It's harder, but much more valuable, to love the things that set us apart from one another. Learning to appreciate our differences brings a new level of intimacy to our relationships with others.

If you listen to two good friends having a conversation, it sounds like two finely tuned musical instruments—they're in perfect pitch with one another.

Iron sharpeneth iron; so a man sharpeneth
the countenance of his friend.

Proverbs 27:17

To My Friend:
The joy of having a friend like
you is a blessing beyond compare.
Our lives are a celebration of
the special bond we share.

We pass through seasons in friendships, just as
we pass through seasons of the year. Our relation-
ships with others grow, bloom, and sometimes
wilt, merely because their time has come. We
don't need to regret these passings, for they are a
natural part of the earth's movement. Instead, we
can look at them with fond recollection, knowing
that spring will soon come.

I count myself in nothing else so happy
As in a soul remembering my good friends.

—William Shakespeare

When our lives get overloaded, one of the first
things we cut back is the time we spend with
friends. But it is these very relationships that can
center us, ease our stress, and remind us of our
true priorities.

We look to our friends for different things.
Some are "night-on-the-town" friends. Some
are telephone friends. Some are office friends.
Some are advice friends. Like colorful blos-
soms, each contributes her unique qualities to
a huge bouquet and brings something special
to our lives.

A best friend absorbs half your sadness
and amplifies twice your joy.

*Ointment and perfume rejoice the heart:
so doth the sweetness of a man's friend by
hearty counsel.*

Proverbs 27:9

*I may not call to talk with you as often as I should.
I may not come to visit you as often as I could.
And even though our busy lives sometimes keep us
apart, no matter how much time goes by, you're
always in my heart.*

*No distance of place or lapse of time can lessen
the friendship of those who are thoroughly persuaded of each other's worth.*

–Robert Southey

*Friendships, like gardens, must be nourished and
cultivated if they are to flourish and thrive. Take
time to pull the weeds, turn the soil, and plant
new seeds. Then enjoy the beauty of this love you
have created.*

Let me be an angel to someone today.
Let me make life easier in some important way.
Let me offer kindness as I go
and cultivate the seeds of hope
so they might bloom and grow.

Let me be a blessing to a stranger or friend.
Let me find a broken heart that I can help
to mend.
Let me offer words of love to those who
know despair
and tend to wounds of others
with compassion, hope, and care.

Let me be an angel to someone in need.
Let me be the bearer of some unexpected deed.
Let me teach the ways of love to everyone I see
and bring the gift of peace to those
who seek serenity.

*Be kindly affectioned on to another with
brotherly love; in honour preferring on another;
Not slothful in business; fervent in spirit;
serving the Lord;
Rejoicing in hope; patient in tribulation;
continuing instant in prayer;
Distributing to the necessity of saints;
given to hospitality.
Bless them which persecute you: bless,
and curse not.*

Romans 12:10–14

*Friendship is a seed planted during
a chance first meeting that grows
into a flower when it's watered
with love. Thank you for tending
our garden of friendship.*

*When we give thanks and praise to someone, we
honor the presence of God in that person. Our
gratitude for the people we love is our acknowledg-
ment of spirit expressing through them.*

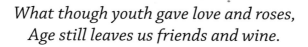

What though youth gave love and roses,
Age still leaves us friends and wine.

—Thomas Moore

The beauty of good friends is that they
can spend long months away from each
other, yet never grow apart.

~~~~~~

Life may tell us that our paths should part,
but God has placed you in my heart.
And though I may not return to you,
our friendship will remain strong and true.

~~~~~~

Give thanks for your friends, each and every day of
your life.

Wherefore comfort yourselves together, and edify one another, even as also ye do.

1 Thessalonians 5:11

A phone call from a friend—a cool drink on a parched, dry day.
A letter from a friend—a break in the clouds when the rain pours down.
A hug from a friend—a down-filled blanket while a snowstorm rages.

Friendship is a flower that blooms through all life's seasons.

We often hesitate to extend help unless asked. We don't want to interfere or overstep our boundaries, or we are afraid that our behavior will be misinterpreted. But an opportunity to assist others is a rare gift, and if your actions come from the heart, you will never be misjudged.

One there is, above all others,
Well deserves the name of Friend;
his is love beyond a brother's,
Costly, free, and knows no end;
They who once his kindness prove
find it everlasting love.
O for grace our hearts to soften!
Teach us, Lord, at length to love;
We, alas! forget too often
What a Friend we have above;
But when home our souls are brought,
We will love You as we ought.

–John Newton,
"One There Is, Above All Others"

True friends are like marathon runners, pacing each other through the race of life. When one stumbles, the other drops back to help. When one surges forward, the other joins in flight.

Sweet is the memory of distant friends! Like the mellow rays of the departing sun, it falls tenderly, yet sadly, on the heart.

—Washington Irving

When you're stuck on the ground,
  friends help you fly.
When you give up,
  friends tell you to try.
When all is dark,
  friends show you the light.
When you stray from your path,
  friends set you right.
Life has its ups and downs, it's true,
  but friends will always be there for you.

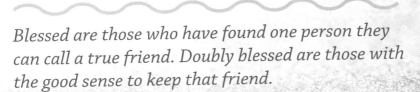

Blessed are those who have found one person they can call a true friend. Doubly blessed are those with the good sense to keep that friend.

When it comes to words of wisdom,
 on these you can depend:
No matter where life takes you,
 it's better with a friend.

Simple pleasures can
become magical when
shared with a friend.

We cannot part with our
friends; we cannot let
our angels go.

–Ralph Waldo Emerson

Just one seemingly simple act of kindness can
have far-reaching consequences. If we stop to
help someone out, we might make their day—or
even make a new friend.

It is my joy in life to find
At every turning of the road
The strong arm of a comrade kind
To help me onward with my load.
And since I have no gold to give,
And love alone must make amends,
My only prayer is, while I live—
God make me worthy of my friends.

–Frank Dempster Sherman

Thank God for friendship. It brings us
joy and comfort and provides refuge
from an often harsh world.

What is so great as friendship, let us carry
with what grandeur of spririt we can. Let
us be silent, so we may hear the whisper of
the gods.

–Ralph Waldo Emerson

There is a fine line between helping each other person and making them dependent on us. We can help a bird with a broken wing by wrapping the injury, but we cannot make that bird fly. That is up to the bird. We can support a friend who wants to go after dream, but we cannot go after that dream for them. That is up to our friend. To truly help another person, we need to guide them to help themselves. Then, and only then, will they be able to become healed, whole, and empowered.

So long as we love we serve; so long as we are loved by others, I would almost say that we are indispensable; and no man is useless while he has a friend.

—Robert Louis Stevenson

Friends like you are a rare treasure. Thank you for all you've done.

Someone to lean on when times get too tough,
someone to laugh with at life's silly stuff,
someone who'll share when there's more than enough,
that's what a friend means to me.

The only way to have a friend is to be one.

–Ralph Waldo Emerson

One of the best things you can say to a friend is simply, "I'll be there for you." Nothing to do, nothing to prove, just the assurance of your presence when they need you. That's exactly what God tells us time and time again in the Bible. He will be there for us.

*And let us consider one another to provoke
unto love and to good works:
Not forsaking the assembling of ourselves
together, as the manner of some is;
but exhorting on another: and so much the
more, as ye see the day approaching.*

Hebrews 10:24–25

*We didn't exactly see eye to eye
As our friendship teetered and years rolled by.
But thanks to the fences you'd always mend
I'm lucky today that you call me friend.*

*Friendships are the golden threads woven into the
tapestries of our lives.*

*May the roof above us never fall in,
and may we friends gathered below
never fall out.*

—Irish Toast

Laughter is the best gift friends can give each other.

A friend loves you at all times. When you aren't looking your best, a friend insists that you do. When you don't feel your best, a friend makes you laugh.

When we love our friends, we see their goodness and beauty, no matter what they look like, how old they are, what they choose to wear. When we learn to recognize the soul underneath these outward trappings, our own lives are enriched.

A true friend is someone who never stops believing in your dreams, even if you have.

When you smile, dear friend, I feel joy in my heart.

And the song, from beginning to end,
I found in the heart of a friend.

—Henry Wadsworth Longfellow

Visiting with old friends is like rereading favorite books. Though you know the stories by heart, you are compelled to turn the pages again and again, reliving the precious memories one more time.

A true friend gives the best advice: not necessarily what you want to hear, but what you need to know.

A friend's smile can warm the winter sky and entice the sun to stay a little longer.

But friendship is precious, not only in the shade, but in the sunshine of life; and thanks to a benevolent arrangement of things, the greater part of life is sunshine.

—*Thomas Jefferson*

I sound much better when I'm singing with my friends, I kick much higher when I'm dancing with my friends, and I laugh much longer when I'm laughing with my friends.

Oh, the comfort—the inexpressible comfort of feeling safe with a person—having neither to weigh thoughts nor measure words, but pouring them all right out, just as they are, chaff and grain together; certain that a faithful hand will take them and sift them, keep what is worth keeping, and then with the breath of kindness blow the rest away.

–Dinah Maria Mulock Craik

Laughing with friends replenishes the soul and warms the heart.

Friendships come about by good fortune, mutual respect, and the grace of God.

*That is, that I may be comforted together with
you by the mutual faith both of you and me.*

Romans 1:12

*For memory has painted this perfect day
With colors that never fade,
And we find at the end of a perfect day
The soul of a friend we've made.*

–Carrie Jacobs Bond

You are forever changed when you find a true friend.

*A true friend laughs at your best funny story no
matter how many times she's heard it.*

*The miracle of friendship usually begins with a
simple smile.*

Ah, how good it feels!
The hand of an old friend.

   —Henry Wadsworth Longfellow

I'd like a little money.
I'd like a little ease.
But a friendship that is faithful
Can outweigh both of these.

Instead of a gem or a flower, cast the gift of a
lovely thought into the heart of a friend.

   —George MacDonald

Barren trees and a chill in the air cannot dispel the
warmth among friends.

Give to your friends unselfishly and freely, and
expect nothing in return but their friendship.

Make no friendship with an angry man; and with a furious man thou shalt not go:
Lest thou learn his ways, and get a snare to thy soul.
Be not thou one of them that strike hands, or of them that are sureties for debts.
If thou hast nothing to pay, why should he take away thy bed from under thee?

Proverbs 22:24-27

It is not good to be alone—even in Paradise.

–Yiddish folk saying

Kind words and thoughtful deeds are celebrated year-round among friends.

Our friendship brings sunshine to the shade, and shade to the sunshine.

–Thomas Burke

Long live the Irish!
Long live their cheer!
Long live our friendship
Year after year!

—Irish Toast

Sweet is the memory of distant friends! Like the mellow rays of the departing sun, it falls tenderly, yet sadly, on the heart.

—Washington Irving

Well, the winter's gone, and I've written no books, earned no fortune; but I've made a friend worth having and I'll try to keep him all my life.

—Louisa May Alcott

Now when Job's three friends heard of all this evil that was come upon him, they came every one from his own place; Eliphaz the Temanite, and Bildad the Shuhite, and Zophar the Naamathite: for they had made an appointment together to come to mourn with him and to comfort him.

And when they lifted up their eyes afar off, and knew him not, they lifted up their voice, and wept; and they rent every one his mantle, and sprinkled dust upon their heads toward heaven.

So they sat down with him upon the ground seven days and seven nights, and none spake a word unto him: for they saw that his grief was very great.

Job 2:11–13

Chapter 10

Hardships & Healing

Be strong and of a good courage, fear not, nor be afraid of them: for the Lord thy God, he it is that doth go with thee; he will not fail thee, nor forsake thee.

Deuteronomy 31:6

Even in our toughest moments, Lord, we yearn to grow into fullest flower. Give us a faith as resilient and determined as dandelions pushing up through cracks in the pavement.

Take this burden from me, Lord,
Free me from this pain.
Let me move with ease and grace
And walk in health again.
Take this yoke upon you, Lord,
And help me toward my goal,
I'm tired of being sick and tired
And long to be made whole.
Release me from my illness
And restore me to my best.
If you can do that for me, Lord,
I'll take care of the rest.

Fear thou not; for I am with thee: be not dismayed; for I am thy God: I will strengthen thee; yea, I will help thee; yea, I will uphold thee with the right hand of my righteousness.

Isaiah 41:10

*E*nliven my imagination, God of new life, so that I can see through today's troubles to coming newness. Surround me with your caring so that I can live as if the new has already begun.

Lord, I am now in tribulation, and my heart is ill at ease, for I am much troubled with the present suffering. . . . Grant me patience, O Lord, even now in this moment. Help me, my God, and then I will not fear, how grievously soever I be afflicted.

—Thomas à Kempis

I am still moving, God, through storms. By your grace—over rough country, you have carried me; amidst pounding waves, you have held me; beyond the horizon of my longings you have shown me your purposes. Even in this small room, sitting still, I am moving, God. Closer.

The righteous cry, and the Lord heareth, and delivereth them out of all their troubles. The Lord is nigh unto them that are of a broken heart; and saveth such as be of a contrite spirit.

Psalm 34:17–18

My Creator, blessed is your presence. For you and you alone give me power to walk through dark valleys into the light again. You and you alone give me hope when there seems no end to my suffering. You and you alone give me peace when the noise of my life overwhelms me. I ask that you give this same power, hope, and peace to all who know discouragement, that they, too, may be emboldened and renewed by your everlasting love. Amen.

*L*ord, my heart was broken, but I know you can fix it. As I learn to depend on you, give me the same thing you gave your servant David: strength and a song. Amen.

*G*od, I look around my community today and I feel helpless. The homeless, the hurting, the needs each one represents are more than I can handle. But you can do it. You can meet each need. Teach me. Strengthen me and use me to serve as I reach out to my neighbor and meet Just One Need at a Time!

*W*hen I feel my control slipping, Lord, I know I only have to call on you for encouragement, direction, and guidance to get your loving assistance.

*T*emptations are everywhere, God. Please stay nearby and keep me strong.

*But the end of all things is at hand: be ye
therefore sober, and watch unto prayer.
And above all things have fervent charity
among yourselves: for charity shall cover
the multitude of sins.*

1 Peter 4:7–8

Lord, I need you here in the midst of this difficult situation, that the very warmth of your love will bring about the resolution and that the brightness of your light will cast out all shadows between us. Amen.

God, hear my prayer. Bless me with patience and a steadfast heart to help me get through such emotionally trying times. Heal the wounds of my heart and soul with the soothing balm of your comforting presence, that I may be able to love and to live again. Amen.

*I*t takes great courage to heal, Lord, great energy to reach out from this darkness to touch the hem of your garment and ask for healing. Bless the brave voices telling nightmare tales of dreadful wounds to the gifted healers of this world. Together, sufferers and healers are binding up damaged parts and laying down burdens carried so long.

*G*od, bless this situation with the gentle, healing power of your love, that I may find the courage to carry on through this dark time of loss and the grace to believe there is happiness ahead. Amen.

*D*ear God, you have sustained me through my illness. You have nursed my injury. You are my true physician, and I glorify you with all my heart. Amen.

God is our refuge and strength, a very present help in trouble.

Psalm 46:1–3

God of my heart, I am a broken person. I do not know how to handle this suffering. I am not strong enough to do it alone. Be my strength, God, and do for me what I simply cannot do for myself. Be the glue that binds the pieces of my shattered soul back together, that I may rise and step back onto the joyful path of life again. Amen.

Despite today's valley of shadow and sickness, I know you, shepherd of my soul, will continue restoring me as I move through treatment to the safe meadow of wellness.

*H*elp me recover from this ambush of illness, Great Physician, and the worry it brings. Reassure my fearful heart that my sickness was never intended; it just happened. Bodies break down, parts age, and minds weary. Your assurance gives me strength to hang on.

*O*f the many ways to suffer, I feel all of them in this firestorm of sadness. It robs my sleep, saps my strengh, and changes me so much I hardly recognize myself. Ease my misery, Lord. Clear my mind as though washing streaks from a window. Hold me when I cry, releasing feelings that keep me sick; send others to hold me, too. Remind me that this pain is temporary and can be relieved, just like my worries.

I'd like to pray to be spared of all pain, but life is full of pain. No one escapes it. Better to ask God to be near whenever it comes.

*S*itting here in this waiting room, O God, time drags and fear festers. Remake worry into energized, active prayers, into trust in the process of healing and recovery. We're scooting over to make room for you, a companion for the waiting.

Why is there so much pain in the world, God? It's so hard to understand. Lord, help us through it all. Help us comprehend or at least simply trust in you.

*N*o darkness is black enough to hide you, Lord, for there is always light even if I sometimes misplace it. Just when I'm ready to give up, there it shines through caregivers, family, friends; through my renewed energy to choose treatments and recovery. I'm absolutely certain you are the sender of this light.

I sought the Lord, and he heard me, and delivered me from all my fears.

Psalm 34:4

$\mathcal{D}$ear God, the pain is so great and unbearable that I feel as though another moment of it will tear me apart. Please rescue me from this pain. Touch my body and heal me. Hear my pleas for only you have the power to deliver me from my affliction. Have mercy upon me. I cry out to you day and night, and I will turn to no one but you.

$\mathcal{L}$ord, the clamor of my life is unbearable. People pressing in on all sides. Decisions crying out to be made. Problems needing to be solved. I don't want to get out of bed in the morning. I want to hide, to escape. Please help me!

$\mathcal{D}$ear Lord, each night the news is full of trouble. So much pain and sorrow. It makes me ache to see it all. Some nights, it seems that's all there is; this world seems sometimes so weary and heavy laden. Then I turn to you and know that you are nearest on the darkest days. And there is comfort in knowing you and that you have not forsaken us or the people whose world is presently dark. Amen.

Lord, we don't like to let stress destroy our even keel, but sometimes it does. We need your wisdom to help us manage the load and your grace to keep us from being ill-tempered.

Thank you, Lord, for helping us through our hard times. You have shown your love for us and made us more compassionate people. Help us show the same love to others who are going through hard times.

My grief feels as if it will never subside, God. Every thing within me melts like wax when I wake up in the morning and realize all over again what has happened. My life is forever changed. Sometimes I wonder if you are there, but I know you have promised always to be with me. Please hold me close. Amen.

Dear God, help me understand that what may appear to be a "goodbye" is really only an "until we meet again." Amen.

Help me grieve and go on...go on in new ways you will reveal to me, Lord, as I make my faltering way as far as I can. Hold me while I name and mourn all I have lost, weeping and wailing like the abandoned child I feel I am. Then, in time and with you to lean on, I can focus on what I have left.

Guard me, guide me angels,
hide me from the troubles all around.
Keep me safe and give me faith to hear
your steps in every sound.

God of my heart, bring me comfort and peace in this time of confusion and sorrow. Help me know that, although things are bleak, there is always a brighter tomorrow.

Give to the winds thy fears
Hope and be undismayed;
God hears thy sighs and counts thy tears
God shall lift up thy head.
Through waves and clouds and storms,
He gently clears thy way.
Wait thou his time; so shall this night
Soon end in joyous day.
Let us in life, death,
They steadfast truth declare
And publish with our latest breath
Thy love and guardian care.

—Paul Gerhardt, translated by John Wesley

In those mysterious, unexplained events of our
lives, we sense the hand of an intervening angel
to remind us of the reality of God's love.

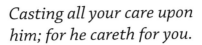

*Casting all your care upon
him; for he careth for you.*

1 Peter 5:7

Lord, although we are often not certain of your intentions when you present us with unpleasant circumstances, we understand that you do have a reason. The hurt isn't just to spite us. Please help us to keep our outlooks positive and allow us to aid others who are as dismayed and in just as much pain as we are. Amen.

Grief, O God of current and tides, is taking me somewhere new. Feeling your guiding hand, I will hold on and keep moving.

*F*ather, you will help us to survive the seasons of surprises in our lives. For just as the harshest winter always gives way to the warm blush of spring, the season of our suffering will give way to a brighter tomorrow, where change becomes a catalyst for new growth and spiritual maturity. Amen.

*G*od, I pray to you today for the healing that only you can bring. I long to be free from pain and suffering, to be whole again in body, mind, and spirit. Give to me the soothing balm of your tender, loving care that I might mount up on wings of eagles and fly with ease again. Amen.

*D*ear God, hear my prayer. I am suffering and in need of your merciful blessings. Please take me into your arms. Give me the courage to keep going through difficult times and the fortitude to move beyond the outer illusions of pain and despair. Only you can heal me, God. In praise and thanks, Amen.

I have set the Lord always before me: because he is at my right hand, I shall not be moved.

Psalm 16:8

Creator God, you have come to me with healing in your hand. When I cried out, you heard me. You provided me with a gift that brought both peace and pleasure to my harried life. You helped me to focus on life instead of illness and sorrow. Lord, thank you for this wondrous gift. Amen.

Dear God, it's not fair. It's hard for me to believe that whatever happens is okay. I want to feel your presence, even if you don't offer a miracle. Please understand how I feel and give me hope.

Heal me, O Lord.
Heal my heart, my soul, my body.
Heal anything in me that is wounded, less than whole.
Then guide me to live in a way that brings healing to others, too.

Comfort, dear God, those whose eyes are filled with tears and those whose backs are near breaking with the weight of a heavy burden. Heal those whose hearts hold a wound and whose faith has been dealt a blow. Bless all who mourn and who despair. Help those who can't imagine how they'll make it through another day. For your goodness and mercy are enough for all the troubles in the world. Amen.

And he said, My presence shall go with thee,
and I will give thee rest.

Exodus 33:14

*L*ord, this healing process is sometimes slow, and I get discouraged and filled with doubt. Can I take this? Will I make it? Yet you always remind me of your powerful presence and assure me that where I am unable to go, you will go for me and what I am unable to do by myself, you will do for me. Thank you, Lord. Amen.

*G*od, we will try to learn and grow from challenges. We pray your promise of a new life can heal our wounds. We will try to remain patient because we know that you will cure us in good time. Amen.

$\mathcal{L}$ord, I know that part of life is loss and that without loss we cannot treasure the new blessings that come our way. But I am still hurting, and the pain is deep. Help me see the beautiful silver lining that surrounds the dark clouds now hanging overhead. Amen.

My Creator, I know in my heart that these tears will one day give way again to joy, yet for now I know only pain. Help me to find the courage to let these tears flow, to feel the loss and heartbreak, so that I may come out whole and cleansed again. For on the other side of my sorrow I know life waits for me. I want to laugh again.

$\mathcal{W}$hen each heartbeat hurts and each breath aches, I pray, God, that you will take some of my blinding pain away. Lift me out of my pain, and give me peace. Amen.

*L*ord, you do not leave us to suffer alone. You are with us in pain, in sickness, and in our worst moments. Thank you for your comfort and healing power. Thank you for getting us through when our bodies fail, when our health falters, and when we need you most of all. Amen.

~~~~~~~~~~~~~~~~~~~~~~~~

O Father, I feel my heart panic. I am so afraid because my world seems to be in such horrible jeopardy. Help me turn to you for courage during this dreadful time. Increase my faith and strengthen my confidence in your care for my welfare. This, I pray. Amen.

These are mean-spirited times, and we quake and shudder. Tend us, loving Creator, and shelter us in the palm of your hand against all that would uproot and destroy us. We are the flowers of your field.

But they that wait upon the
Lord shall renew their strength;
they shall mount up with wings as eagles;
they shall run, and not be weary; and they
shall walk and not faint.

Isaiah 40:31

While I wait for this piercing pain of loneli-
ness to pass, Great Comforter, cradle me as the
wailing, lost child I've become. Closing my eyes
and breathing deeply, I feel your warming pres-
ence as a blanket tossed around my shoulders
and know that no matter how lost I feel right
now, you hold the most important truth, whis-
pering it now: "You are my beloved child. I am
with you."

eavenly Father, you say that you will heal me. Please help me realize there are different forms of healing. While your healing is sometimes miraculous and other times almost common and everyday, your healing in on occasion invisible. These are moments when life doesn't seem to change, and I have to look inside to find a place of acceptance. It is in this place where I am reminded that who I am is separate from the pain that invades my life. Please help me to turn my thoughts to you. Amen.

Abide in peace, knowing that this is not the first time such trouble has entered the human race. And it is not the kind of crisis that makes a difference to life and death. It will not shed blood or cause great suffering.

Yes, it is a problem—with the one, primary quality that characterizes all such tribulations: They all, eventually, come to an end.

O God, healing is going so-o-o-o slowly, and I am impatient and grumpy. Mind, body, or soul, this could take a long time. Remind me that recovery is a journey, not a hasty jet-lagged arrival. Bless me with faith to sustain me, step by small step. You do miraculous things with faith as tiny as mustard seeds that, in time, blossom into awesome growth. I hold that picture as I make mustard-seed progress along the road to healing.

*So shall they fear the name of the
Lord from the west, and his glory from
the rising of the sun. When the enemy
shall come in like a flood, the Spirit
of the Lord shall lift up a standard
against him.*

Isaiah 59:19

*Thank you, Lord, for reddened eyes. Believing
your promise that comfort follows mourning,
we bawl and sob. In your wisdom, onion-peeling
salty tears differ from cleansing grieving ones;
we're grateful for their healing. Deliver us from
stiff upper lips, and if we've lost our tears, help
us find them.*

I don't want to do it all today,
Lord. I want to leave undone that
which fails to serve you, and leave
unsaid that which fails to glorify you.

*L*oving Jesus, Healer of the Sick, I place in your hands myself and all who need your healing. Help us crave the healing that only you can give. May we not define what that healing should be, but accept your gift of abundant life however you give it to us. In your way, in your time, restore us to full health and wholeness. Amen.

$\mathcal{L}$ord, only you can comfort us when we grieve. The heaviness we feel at such times can make even breathing a struggle. But you, O Lord, stay close. You fill us with your peace and your comfort. You never let us retreat completely from your light into the darkness of despair. And finally, in your time, you restore joy to our souls. We are ever so grateful, O Great Comforter.

So many terrors and troubles confront us, so many dangers and calamities. Is anyone ever completely safe? Only when we trust God, do we know peace and assurance in the shelter of his care.

~~~~~~~~~~

When disaster strikes our lives, God is our rock, and nothing can separate us from him. Indeed, nothing can separate us from his love.

~~~~~~~~~~

When someone we love is trapped in a prison of defeat and discouragement, we can help them break free of the chains that bind them by doing these three things: supporting their deepest dreams, believing in their gifts and talents, and loving and accepting them for who they are at this very moment.

*L*ord, send me an angel to guide me and guard me, to lead and direct me, to comfort and hold me.

Send me an angel who knows what my heart needs most and who always has the highest and best solutions to my most challenging problems.

Send me an angel to walk with me through the dark and hold my hand as I tread the rocky road of life.

Send me an angel soon, Lord.

Amen

These hard times help me see with new eyes, Lord. Despite my tears, I see more clearly your tender mercies, my great need for your presence, and the angels in my life I had overlooked or would never have otherwise seen. Thank you for opening my eyes, even as you comfort my heart.

You know, Lord, lately I have been struggling just to get through the next hour, minute, second. Be merciful to me in my weakness and bring me strength and encouragement through the angels you send, faithful messengers of your compassion and comfort. Amen

May I be blessed in this suffering. May I know that you can use this thing to show me a mistaken attitude, a destructive behavior. In that way, may I be blessed in this suffering, O Lord, my God.

When life seems darkest and we feel lost and all alone, that is when we are most surrounded by angels who care for us. All we need to do is open our hearts to see them reaching out to us with love.

*L*ord, once again I am aware that you, by your grace, gave me the strength to work through a situation that I was woefully unprepared to face. I accept that when we are completely out of ideas, drained of all energy, and so sick at heart we can barely breathe, your grace and strength lift us up and carry us forward. Thank you, Lord.

*W*hen grief fills my heart, Father, whether I'm feeling loss, shame, betrayal, or some other sorrow, I know it's temporary, even though at times it feels as though it will never go away. I know that your future for me is joy, and when it comes, I will not reject it. Strengthen me with your joy today, Father. I need it to lift up my soul.

Have not I commanded thee? Be strong and of a good courage; be not afraid, neither be thou dismayed: for the Lord thy God is with thee whithersoever thou goest.

Joshua 1:9

There is no greater comfort to a broken spirit than the love of God. There is no more soothing a balm to heal the wounds of a suffering soul than the love of God. There is no deeper peace to be found for a restless heart than the love of God.

I feel an old familiar panic coming over me, Lord. Comfort me now. As I breathe deeply, fill me with the knowledge that you are present and you are in control. Thank you, Lord. Only your intervention can calm my troubled soul.

*D*ear Lord, we live in a broken world. We need your touch. Heal us of our prejudices, our sicknesses, our compulsions, our hatreds, and our shortsightedness. Help us to see people as you see them. For that matter, help us see ourselves as you see us. Teach us to treat life as the gift you meant it to be. Keep us safe. Make us whole. Give us love to spare and forgiveness that can only come from you. Amen.

Lighten our darkness, Lord, we pray; and in your mercy defend us from all perils and dangers of this night; for the love of your only Son, our Savior Jesus Christ. Amen.

—Gelasian Sacramentary, "An Evening Prayer"

When trouble strikes, O God, we are restored by small signs of hope found in ordinary places: friends, random kindness, shared pain and support. Help us collect them like mustard seeds that can grow into a spreading harvest of well-being.

God's blessing of joy replaces our sorrow.

> *Keep me at evening,*
> *Keep me at morning,*
> *Keep me at noon,*
> *I am tired,*
> *astray and stumbling, shield me from sin.*

> —Celtic Prayer

Left alone now, we drift aimlessly like untied balloons let loose to fly helter-skelter. Yet life goes on, decisions must be made. O God, help us make up minds that won't stay still. Give us good sense to put off until tomorrow what we shouldn't try today. Reassure us this is only temporary, a brief hesitation, not a giving up; hold up a mirror for us to see a once-again clear-eyed person.

Sweet hour of prayer, sweet hour of prayer,
That calls me from a world of care
And bids me at my Father's throne
Make all my wants and wishes known!
In seasons of distress and grief,
My soul has often found relief,
And oft escaped the tempter's snare
By thy return, sweet hour of prayer.

—William Walford

Calm me enough, O Lord, to breathe deeply and restoratively despite my racing heart, pounding headache, and generally fatigued body and mind. Prayer restores me in the presence of all that threatens to undo me, which I name to you now.

Touch and calm my turbulent emotions, God of the still waters. Whisper words to the listening ears of my soul. In hearing your voice, give me assurance beyond a shadow of a doubt that you are my companion in life, eternally.

God promises us his comfort, but he also uses us as his agents to comfort others. In fact, the difficulties we've gone through often give us the ability to reassure others who are now going through the same experiences. How will God use you to extend comfort to someone else?

Storms sometimes arrive in our lives with hurricane-force winds. We feel as if our hearts are caught in the vortex. But just when we think we'll be destroyed, a still, small voice appears in the eye of the storm to remind us that we are not alone.

Though we may not think there is something to gain in the depths of despair, it is only when we begin to heal that we finally see the truth.

As above the darkest storm cloud
Shines the sun, serenely bright
Waiting to restore to nature
All the glory of his light,
So, behind each cloud of sorrow,
So, in each affliction, stands,
Hid, an angel, with a blessing
From the Father in his hand.

–Daniel H. Howard

Whatever tests in life you're facing, whether it's a challenge of relationships, finances, or your career, the loving Spirit that created you is always available to guide you into a better life.

If I'm honest with myself, I'll admit that the greatest joys in my life have sprung from the fertile grounds of suffering—but only after I have asked God to take charge of my garden of sorrow.

Remember to turn to God for help, for in him there is rescue, refuge, and peace.

And the peace of God, which passeth all understanding, shall keep your hearts and minds through Christ Jesus.

Philippians 4:7

Father in heaven, sometimes I feel anger welling up inside me, and I need to turn to you for counsel. Please stay near to me and help me to find ways to express my emotions without harming another's feelings or getting myself so upset I cannot see past my own feelings. I need to understand myself, express myself, and accept myself—all within the bounds of your teachings. Amen.

We have been created to love each other, to help each other, and to heal each other. In doing so, we love, help, and heal ourselves.

The present tragedy is so overwhelming, O God. Please give me eyes of faith to see change and healing. Amen.

We are grateful, O God, for glimpses we are given of you during times like these. Thank you for showing us how, during raging winds, the mother cardinal refuses to move, standing like a mighty shelter over the fledglings beneath her wings. Secure us in the truth that we, the children of your heart, are likewise watched over and protected during life's storms.

Father, hold us in your arms in the midst of devastation and ruin. Remind us that rampaging nature and human evil will not touch us in our eternal homes. Send your angels to remind us that our lives and homes on earth are part of the journey, not our final destination. Amen.

Gently, Lord
Love me gently.
I'm hurting now.
I've lived to see your sovereignty
You've taught my knees to bow.
I've caught glimpses of your glory.
I've seen your righteous ways.
But right now I need you, Father,
Just to face another day.

God, how much longer must I stay curled up in a ball behind this large stone, seeking protection from the storm that swirls around me? I have watched the weeds bow and bend and still not break against the onslaught of the wind. God, I sense I must bend and bow in the midst of the strong forces that pummel me. Then I will find strength to endure until the morning light comes, when I will stand once again because of your help.

*G*od, sometimes I wish I could be saved from the struggle and pain of learning the hard way. But, Lord, that's not your plan, and I need to be willing to wait as you work gently from the inside out. Please grant me some strength in this time of uncertainty. I trust and love you. Amen.

How often we look upon God as our last and feeblest resource! We go to him because we have nowhere else to go. And then we learn that the storms of life have driven us, not upon the rocks, but into the desired haven.

–George MacDonald

When we see our enemies from God's perspective, compassion follows, for He has seen the sorrows in their hearts that have caused them to behave in such a manner. He longs to reach out to these people and comfort them, and He sometimes uses our hands to do it.

Submit yourselves therefore to God.
Resist the devil, and he will flee from you.

James 4:7

Through the darkest days, God walks beside me and will never leave me. His presence comforts me and gives me the courage to keep going no matter what the circumstances are.

Through the darkest days,
God walks beside us.

When someone breaks our heart, we mourn, we grieve, and we feel the pain of rejection. We pray to God for healing and relief. And then we pick up the pieces and, with God's help and guidance, rebuild a heart that is even stronger, more resilient, and ready to love again.

When drooping pleasure turns to grief,
And trembling faith is changed to fear,
The murmuring wind, the quivering leaf,
Shall softly tell us, Thou are near!

—Oliver Wendell Holmes, Sr.

Your soul can dance though the pain is here.
Call healing music to your ear.
Spot emotion's fickle turning,
Leap in love,
Stretch hopes,
Master fear's deep strains.
Dare to dance both health and pain.
However clumsy, long, or fleeting,
We dance life well if grace is leading.

When your heart is empty, filling it with
happy memories can help.

Chapter 11

Life

Jesus said unto her, I am the resurrection, and the life: he that believeth in me, though he were dead, yet shall he live:

And whosoever liveth and believeth in me shall never die. Believest thou this?

John 11:25–26

And whatsoever ye do, do it heartily,
as to the Lord, and not unto men;
Knowing that of the Lord ye shall receive
the reward of the inheritance: for ye
serve the Lord Christ.

Colossians 3:23–24

The beauty of creation inspires me to live a life where I, too, can create something beautiful.

May you celebrate this day with all your heart. Rejoice in the beauty of its light and warmth. Give thanks for the air and grass and sidewalks. Let gratitude for other faces flow into your soul. And cherish the chance to work and play, to think and speak—knowing this: All simple pleasures are opportunities for praise.

Life is real! Life is earnest!
And the grave is not its goal;
Dust thou art, to dust returnest;
Was not spoken of the soul.

–Henry Wadsworth Longfellow,
"A Psalm of Life"

Take time to reflect on the people and things around you. It is in these quiet moments that inspiration grows and we recognize the miracle of life.

Life is like a jigsaw puzzle. When you look at each individual piece, it makes little sense. But when the pieces are all put in their proper place, the end result is a beautiful image, whole and complete. Thus the individual events of your life may make little sense at the time they occur, but when viewed as part of the "big picture," they make all the sense in the world.

To be with God, there is no need to be continually in church. We may make [a chapel] of our heart wherein to return from time to time to converse with him in meekness, humility, and love. There is not in the world a kind of life more sweet and delightful than that of a continual conversation with God.

—Brother Lawrence

I do not want my life to be perceived as nothing more than noise, but as beautiful music that inspires, soothes, and uplifts.

*In him was life; and the life
was the light of men.*

John 1:4

*One ought, every day at least, to hear a
little song, read a good poem, see a fine
picture, and, if it were possible, to speak a
few reasonable words.*

–Johann Wolfgang von Goethe

*Nothing great was ever accomplished by
sitting in the stands. In order to experience
life fully, you must get into the race and
risk being bumped, sidelined, and put out of
commission for a while. But at least you will
have tried. At least you will have dared. At
least you will have dreamed.*

Being in the flow of life means letting things happen in their own natural timing. When you try to force things to happen, you're met with resistance, and you run up against numerous obstacles. You end up taking detours that waste your time and energy, and your enthusiasm wanes as the task becomes more difficult. Often you end up making something happen, only to find that is wasn't what you really wanted to have happen! But if you just relax and go with the flow of life, the natural order of things takes over, and divine timing kicks into gear. Life becomes effortless, harmonious, and enjoyable, just as it was meant to be.

The real voyage of discovery lies not in seeking new landscapes but in having new eyes.

—Marcel Proust

And God said, Let the waters bring forth abundantly the moving creature that hath life, and fowl that may fly above the earth in the open firmament of heaven.

Genesis 1:20

One person who has mastered life is better than a thousand persons who have mastered only the contents of books, but no one can get anything out of life without God.

—Meister Eckhardt

Life becomes much easier and more enjoyable when we know we are never alone. We always have our Higher Power to turn to for strength, hope, guidance, and renewal. God is on the job 24 hours a day, 7 days a week, 365 days a year.

*Live all you can; it's a mistake not to.
It doesn't so much matter what you do in
particular, so long as you have your life. If you
haven't had that what have you had? What
one loses one loses; make no mistake about
that. The right time is any time that one is
still so lucky as to have. Live!*

–Henry James

*I'm getting a crick in my neck trying to see around
the bend, God of past and future. I'm wearing myself out second guessing. Teach me to live in today,
needing just a small glimpse down the road. No
need to borrow trouble that may not be waiting.*

*Life consists not in holding good cards
but in playing those you hold well.*

–Josh Billings

*O*Lord, bless our life stages, for they read like growth rings on a mighty tree: our beginnings and firsts with their excitement, newness, and anxiety; our middles, full of diligence and commitment and, yes, we confess, sometimes boredom, but also risk and derring-do; our "nexts," the harvests and reapings; the slowing down and freedom. In your hands this time can be rich and full like an overflowing cup, not a last or a final or an empty or an ending stage at all. You are an Alpha and Omega God, the parentheses between which we live, move, and have our being. Bless our comings and goings.

When we are unable to find tranquility within ourselves, it is useless to seek it elsewhere.

—François, Duc de La Rochefoucauld

I expect to pass through this world but once. Any good therefore that I can do, or any kindness that I can show to my fellow-creature, let me do it now. Let me not defer or neglect it, for I shall not pass this way again.

—Stephen Grellet

God may throw us a few curves in life—we may feel hassled, troubled, anxious, or uncomfortable, and not understand why our circumstances don't fit our desires. But if we trust in the wisdom of his plan, God will provide for all our needs.

Let me but live my life from year to year,
With forward face and unreluctant soul;
Not hurrying to, nor turning from, the goal;
Not mourning for the things that disappear
In the dim past, nor holding back in fear
From what the future veils; but with a whole
And happy heart, that pays its toll
To youth and age, and travels on with cheer.

—Henry Van Dyke

A life of compassion toward others is a life of
reverence toward Christ

But well for him whose feet hath trod
The weary road of toil and strife,
Yet from the sorrows of his life
Builds ladders to be nearer God.

—Oscar Wilde, "A Lament"

*For the life of the flesh is in the blood:
and I have given it to you upon the
altar to make an atonement for your
souls: for it is the blood that maketh
an atonement for the soul.*

Leviticus 17:14

*All life is an experiment. The more
experiments you make the better.*

–Ralph Waldo Emerson

How easily, O God of eternity, for us to assume our time
is like the grains of sand on an ocean beach—vast and endless.
Remind us that each of our lives is limited like the sand in the
hourglass. May what we do with that sand, play in it, work in it,
build our relationships, whatever, be wise use of this precious
gift of living.

From each of life's misfortunes, large or small, comes a new beginning, an opportunity to renew your faith in the future.

The world holds so many priceless things— the falling rain, a rose in bloom, the wind that sings, an oyster's pearl, the mustard seed. If we can cherish just one precious gift, our lives will be rich indeed.

Treasured memories form a basis for today's choices, and by using faith's discernment, I've learned what matters and what lasts.

Think of each problem you encounter as nothing more than a challenging reminder from God to think a little higher and reach a little farther. When met with a difficult situation along the road of life, greet it, acknowledge it, and move past it. Then you will be able to continue on your journey a little stronger, a little wiser.

Life with faith has meaning and purpose. It transforms the smallest actions into elements of significance, contributing to a better world.

Most of us realize that we are naturally self-centered, and we often respond to those around us in ways that make us appear proud, haughty, or arrogant. But if we look at Jesus' life, we see an excellent example of humility—an example that we should strive to follow. He taught that pride was destructive, but humility was powerful. Rather than touting his own greatness, Jesus was willing to kneel down and wash the feet of others, to show that we should all be servants to each other—and to God.

A man should have the fine point of his soul taken off to become fit for this world.

–John Keats

*Abide thou with me, fear not:
for he that seeketh my life seeketh thy life:
but with me thou shalt be in safeguard.*

1 Samuel 22:23

When one door closes another door opens; but we often look so long and so regretfully upon the closed door that we do not see the one which has opened for us.

–Alexander Graham Bell

You can reach the end of one road, but you never come to the end of the line.

He asked life of thee, and thou gavest it him,
even length of days for ever and ever.

Psalm 21:4

Inspired by you, Great God, and grateful for the unique gifts we're discovering, we toss ourselves into the stream of life to make ripples wherever we are. In your hands, our gifts can offer a gift that keeps on making ever-widening circles to reach all those stranded on shore.

A happy attitude is food for the spirit. Staying in God's grace makes the challenges of life a little easier. Lessons are learned with less effort. Mercy is given more freely. Joy returns!

Blessed is he who expects nothing, for he shall never be disappointed.

–Jonathan Swift

A wise person once said to live each day as though you might die tomorrow. But you should also live each day as though you might live forever.

The meaning I picked, the one that most changed my life: Ovecome fear, behold wonder.

–Aeschylus

We make our own plans, but it is God who leads the way and clears the obstacles from our path.

When I am wrong, I turn within to find the right way. God's eternal wisdom is like a flowing river I can tap into at any time, especially when I am clueless and don't know which way to turn. I take comfort in knowing I don't have to be a genius and figure out every last detail

of my life. God knows best, and as long as I stay in tune with his word, I will be divinely inspired.

Life is beyond our control. That is precisely why angels guard us.

One day when we face these beings
of light who have guided our path
and done God's work in our life, we
will wonder how we ever overlooked
their presence.

Grow old along with me!
The best is yet to be,
The last of life, for which the first was made;
Our times are in his hand
Who saith, "A whole I planned,
Youth shows but half;
trust God:
See all, nor be afraid."

—Robert Browning

If you really don't miss someone or someplace, you're not living life deeply enough.

Lord, I wish to live a long life, but I fear growing old. I want to accomplish great things, but I fear risking what I already have. I desire to love with all my heart, but the prospect of self-revelation makes me shrink back. Perhaps for just this day, you would help me reach out? Let me bypass these dreads and see instead your hand reaching back to mine—right now—just as it always has.

*To every thing there is a season, and a time to
every purpose under the heaven:
A time to be born, and a time to die, a time to
plant, and a time to pluck up that which is planted;
A time to kill, and a time to heal; a time to break
down, and a time to build up;
A time to weep, and a time to laugh; a time to
mourn, and a time to dance;
A time to cast away stones, and a time to gather
stones together; a time to embrace, and a time to
refrain from embracing;
A time to get, and a time to lose; a time to keep,
and a time to cast away;
A time to rend, and a time to sew; a time to keep
silence, and a time to speak;
A time to love, and a time to hate; a time of war,
and a time of peace.*

Ecclesiastes 3:1–8

Dost thou love life? Then do not squander time; for that's the stuff life is made of.

—Benjamin Franklin

Intelligence can be measured by certificates on your wall or books you have read, but, in the end, all that knowledge pales in comparison to the wisdom gained when you truly participate in life.

Each life that touches ours for good is a reflection of God's love for us.

*I*n a moment of quiet, dark stillness, or even in the bustle of daily life, you may occasionally feel that you are in the company of an angel. Revel in its divine presence!

O God, we give thanks that your son Jesus Christ, who has shared our earthly life, has now ascended to prepare our heavenly life. Grant that, through coming to know him by faith on earth, we may come to know him by sight in heaven.

–The Gelasian Sacramentary

I call heaven and earth to record this day against you, that I have set before you life and death, blessing and cursing: therefore choose life, that both thou and thy seed may live: That thou mayest love the Lord thy God, and that thou mayest obey his voice, and that thou mayest cleave unto him: for he is thy life, and the length of thy days: that thou mayest dwell in the land which the Lord sware unto thy fathers, to Abraham, to Isaac, and to Jacob, to give them.

Deuteronomy 30:19–20

Truth is as impossible to be soiled by any outward touch as the sunbeam.

–John Milton

When you are in the midst of suffering, time is too slow. When you are in the midst of excitement, time moves too quickly. Only in the present moment does times cease to exist. True happiness is found there, in the now, where regrets of the past and the fears of the future give way to the bliss of just being alive.

The person who has lived the most is not the one with the most years but the one with the richest experiences.

–Jean Jacques Rousseau, Emile

There is another thing that we of middle life need to guard against, and that is the loss of early enthusiasms and ideals. The tendency of life's actualities is to sober and sometimes embitter. It is a difficult thing to experience trial and failure, to see the hollowness and shame, the trickery and cruelty of the social, commercial, political world, and not get cynical and skeptical—to lose, if not your faith in God, what is next worse, your faith in man and interest in man. It is hard, in contact with the actual world to preserve your faith in an ideal world, your ardor in its pursuit. The youthful vision fades, romance gives way to prosy plodding, and life's springtime grows into the hot, dusty parched summer. Oh, men and women of riper years, let us not fail to carry our earlier enthusiasms into the dry details, the grave responsibilities of later life and make the desert places rejoice and blossom as the rose!

–Charles Sumner Hoyt,
The Octave of Life

The thief cometh not, but for to steal, and to kill, and to destroy: I am come that they might have live, and that they might have it more abundantly.

John 10:10

How joyful life becomes when we surrender to our faith in God, allowing his will to work through us. We give up resistance and frustration, and things suddenly seem to flow with greater ease. We still have obstacles, but also the strength and resources to overcome them. Living in faith and experiencing more peace and joy is what God intended for us!

Life is a gift to be used every day,
Not to be smothered and hidden away;
It isn't a thing to be stored in a chest
Where you gather your keepsakes and
treasure your best;
It isn't a joy to be sipped now and then
And promptly put back in a dark place again.
Life is a gift that the humblest may boast of
And one that the humblest may well
make the most of.
Get out and live it each hour of the day,
Wear it and use it as much as you may;
Don't keep it in niches and corners and grooves,
You'll find that in service its beauty improves.

–Edgar A. Guest

*A*s you look at your own life, how might you be an angel to others? How might you pattern your life as to inspire others to greater heights in their own loving and giving?

God asks no man whether he will accept life. That is not the choice. You must take it. The only choice is how.

—Henry Ward Beecher

See then that ye walk circumspectly,
not as fools, but as wise,
Redeeming the time, because
the days are evil.

Ephesians 5:15-16

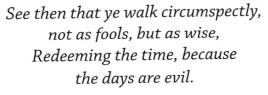

Faith is my soul's good friend that urges me
on, convincing me I will victoriously reach the
finish line in this race called my life.

There is only the gift of the moment. Savor it.
It is a gift.

–Anonymous

Jesus Christ is the true source of new life.

No day should ever be so hectic that there is not time in it for solitude and reflection.

Certain days, certain events come bounding into our way to remind us of how out of control life really is. It is then that we are most grateful for the angels that guard our way and guide our paths.

God's highest priority is that we get to know him and live a life that reflects his love and justice.

For he that will love life, and see good days,
let him refrain his tongue from evil, and his lips
that they speak no guile:
Let him eschew evil, and do good;
let him seek peace, and ensue it.
For the eyes of the Lord are over the righteous,
and his ears are open unto their prayers: but the
face of the Lord is against them that do evil.

1 Peter 3:10–12

Loving Jesus is not something that happens auto-
matically. It is not something that's easy or natural.
It is learned through the trials of life.

Carpe Diem! Rejoice while
you are alive; Enjoy the day;
live life to the fullest; Make
the most of what you have.
It is later than you think.

–Horace

Do all things without
murmurings and disputings:
That ye may be blameless and harmless,
the sons of God, without rebuke, in the midst
of a crooked and perverse nation, among
whom ye shine as lights in the world;
Holding forth the word of life; that I may
rejoice in the day of Christ, that I have not run
in vain, neither laboured in vain.
Yea, and if I be offered upon the sacrifice and
service of your faith, I joy,
and rejoice with you all.
For the same cause also do ye joy,
and rejoice with me.

Philippians 2:14–18

Faith in a wise and trustworthy God, even in broken times like these, teaches us a new math: subtracting old ways and adding new thoughts because sharing with God divides our troubles and multiplies unfathomable possibilities for renewed life.

Christ, the blessed one, gives to all
Wonderful words of life;
Sinner heed now his loving call,
Wonderful words of life.
All so freely given,
Wooing us to heaven:
Beautiful words, wonderful words
Wonderful words of life.

—Phillip P. Bliss